OSBORNE REVISE!

ACCA

ACCA F2 Management Accounting

NOTES

Published by Osborne Books Limited

Unit 2
The Business Centre
Molly Millars Lane
Wokingham
Berkshire RG41 2QZ

Tel 01905 748071

Email books@osbornebooks.co.uk

Website www.osbornebooks.co.uk

Printed and bound in Great Britain.

British Library Cataloguing in Publication Data

A catalogue record for this book is available from the British Library

ISBN 978-1-911198-22-2

CONTENTS

HOW TO USE THESE *ACCA Notes*

These *ACCA Notes* have been designed to help you to:

- **Renew** your approach to syllabus areas that might not have been clear first time around. Use them to supplement your learning and to help you to clarify details of the syllabus of which you are unsure. It is easy to look things up using the detailed index and contents page and find quickly the topic you need help with

- **Refresh** topics you have covered before but may have forgotten. If it is a while since you studied a topic which underpins a higher level subject that you now need to study, for example, use them as a refresher tool to remind yourself of what you have already learnt

- **Revise** and make the best use of your time before your examinations. Take advantage of the summarised topics, learning summaries, summary diagrams, key points, definitions and exam tips to support your revision in the critical period leading up to your real exam.

PREPARING FOR THE EXAM

To pass your exam you need an understanding of the syllabus and exam technique is vital. These *ACCA Notes* follow the syllabus with succinct coverage, offering tips on how to get the best results in the exam.

ACCA Notes – ICONS

LEARNING SUMMARY

The 'learning summary' provides details of the key learning objectives of each section of content.

DEFINITION

The 'definition' boxes highlight and explain key terms.

KEY POINT

The 'key point' boxes emphasise key points which are fundamental to your understanding of the syllabus.

> ## Do you understand?
>

The 'do you understand' boxes contain short form questions which are not necessarily exam style, but which test that you have understood the core syllabus content before you progress onto exam style questions.

PAPER INFORMATION

The aim of ACCA Paper F2, Management accounting/FIA Diploma in Accounting and Business, Management accounting, is to develop knowledge and understanding of management accounting techniques to support management in planning, controlling and monitoring performance in a variety of business context.

SYLLABUS

A   THE NATURE, SOURCE AND PURPOSE OF MANAGEMENT INFORMATION

(1)   Accounting for management

(a)   Describe the purpose and role of cost and management accounting within an organisation.[k] **Ch 1**

(b)   Compare and contrast financial accounting with cost and management accounting.[k] **Ch 1**

(c)   Outline the managerial processes of planning, decision making and control.[k] **Ch 1**

(d)   Explain the difference between strategic, tactical and operational planning.[k] **Ch 1**

(e)   Distinguish between data and information.[k] **Ch 1**

(f)   Identify and explain the attributes of good information.[k] **Ch 1**

(g)   Explain the limitations of management information in providing guidance for managerial decision-making.[k] **Ch 1**

(2)   Sources of data

(a)   Describe sources of information from within and outside the organisation (including government statistics, financial press, professional or trade associations, quotations and price list).[k] **Ch 2**

(b)   Explain the uses and limitations of published information/data (including information from the internet).[k] **Ch 2**

(c)   Describe the impact of general economic environment on costs/revenues.[k] **Ch 2**

(d)   Explain sampling techniques (random, systematic, stratified, multistage, cluster and quota).[k] **Ch 2**

(e)   Choose an appropriate sampling method in a specific situation. (Note: Derivation of random samples will not be examined).[s] **Ch 2**

(3)   Cost classification

(a)   Explain and illustrate production and non-production costs. [k] **Ch 4**

(b)   Describe the different elements of non production costs – administrative, selling, distribution and finance.[k] **Ch 4**

(c)   Describe the different elements of production cost – materials, labour and overheads.[k] **Ch 4**

(d)   Explain the importance of the distinction between production and non-production costs when valuing output and inventories.[k] **Ch 4**

(e)   Explain and illustrate with examples classifications used in the analysis of the product/service costs including by function, direct and indirect, fixed and variable, stepped fixed and semi variable costs.[s] **Ch 4**

(f)   Explain and illustrate the use of codes in categorising transaction.[k] **Ch 4**

(g) Describe and illustrate, graphically, different types of cost behaviour.[s] **Ch 4**

(h) Use high/low analysis to separate the fixed and variable elements of total costs including situations involving semi variable and stepped fixed costs and changes in the variable cost per unit.[s] **Ch 4**

(i) Explain the structure of linear functions and equations.[s] **Ch 4**

(j) Explain and illustrate the concept of cost objects, cost units and cost centres.[s] **Ch 4**

(k) Distinguish between cost, profit, investment and revenue centres.[k] **Ch 1**

(l) Describe the differing needs for information of cost, profit, investment and revenue centre managers.[k] **Ch 1**

(4) Presenting information

(a) Prepare written reports representing management information in suitable formats according to purpose.[s] **Ch 3**

(b) Present information using table, charts and graphs (bar charts, line graphs, pie charts and scatter graphs).[s] **Ch 3**

(c) Interpret information (including the above tables, charts and graphs) presented in management reports.[s] **Ch 3**

B COST ACCOUNTING METHODS AND SYSTEMS

(1) Accounting for material, labour and overheads

(a) Accounting for materials

(i) Describe the different procedures and documents necessary for the ordering, receiving and issuing of materials from inventory.[k] **Ch 5**

(ii) Describe the control procedures used to monitor physical and 'book' inventory and to minimise discrepancies and losses.[k] **Ch 5**

(iii) Interpret the entries and balances in the material inventory account.[s] **Ch 5**

(iv) Identify, explain and calculate the costs of ordering and holding inventory (including buffer inventory).[s] **Ch 5**

(v) Calculate and interpret optimal reorder quantities.[s] **Ch 5**

(vi) Calculate and interpret optimal reorder quantities when discounts apply.[s] **Ch 5**

(vii) Produce calculations to minimise inventory costs when inventory is gradually replenished.[s] **Ch 5**

(viii) Describe and apply appropriate methods for establishing reorder levels where demand in the lead time is constant. [s] **Ch 5**

(ix) Calculate the value of closing inventory and material issues using LIFO, FIFO and average methods.[s] **Ch 5**

(b) Accounting for labour

(i) Calculate direct and indirect costs of labour.[s] **Ch 6**

(ii) Explain the methods used to relate input labour costs to work done.[k] **Ch 6**

(iii) Prepare the journal and ledger entries to record labour cost inputs and outputs.[s] **Ch 6**

(iv) Describe different remuneration methods: time-based systems, piecework systems and individual and group incentive schemes.[k] **Ch 6**

(v) Calculate the level, and analyse the costs and causes of labour turnover.[s] **Ch 6**

(vi) Explain and calculate labour efficiency, capacity and production volume ratios.[s] **Ch 6**

(vii) Interpret the entries in the labour account.[s] **Ch 6**

(c) Accounting for overheads

(i) Explain the different treatment of direct and indirect expenses.[k] **Ch 7**

(ii) Describe the procedures involved in determining production overhead absorption rates.[k] **Ch 7**

(iii) Allocate and apportion production overheads to cost centres using an appropriate basis.[s] **Ch 7**

(iv) Reapportion service cost centre costs to production cost centres (including using the reciprocal method where service cost centres work for each other).[s] **Ch 7**

(v) Select, apply and discuss appropriate bases for absorption rates.[s] **Ch 7**

(vi) Prepare journal and ledger entries for manufacturing overheads incurred and absorbed.[s] **Ch 7**

(vii) Calculate and explain the under and over absorption of overheads.[s] **Ch 7**

(2) Absorption and marginal costing

(a) Explain the importance of, and apply, the concept of contribution.[s] **Ch 8**

(b) Demonstrate and discuss the effect of absorption and marginal costing on inventory valuation and profit determination.[s] **Ch 8**

(c) Calculate profit or loss under absorption and marginal costing.[s] **Ch 8**

(d) Reconcile the profits or losses calculated under absorption and marginal costing.[s] **Ch 8**

(e) Describe the advantages and disadvantages of absorption and marginal costing.[k] **Ch 8**

(3) Costing methods

(a) Job and batch costing

(i) Describe the characteristics of job and batch costing.[k] **Ch 9**

(ii) Describe the situations where the use of job or batch costing would be appropriate.[k] **Ch 9**

(iii) Prepare cost records and accounts in job and batch costing situations.[k] **Ch 9**

(iv) Establish job and batch costs from given information.[s] **Ch 9**

Note: Situations involving work in process and losses in the same process are excluded.

(b)   Process costing

    (i)   Describe the characteristics of process costing.[k] **Ch 9**

    (ii)   Describe the situations where the use of process costing would be appropriate.[s] **Ch 9**

    (iii)   Explain the concepts of normal and abnormal losses and abnormal gains.[k] **Ch 9**

    (iv)   Calculate the cost per unit of process outputs.[s] **Ch 9**

    (v)   Prepare process accounts involving normal and abnormal losses and abnormal gains.[s] **Ch 9**

    (vi)   Calculate and explain the concept of equivalent units.[s] **Ch 9**

    (vii)   Apportion process costs between work remaining in process and transfers out of a process using the weighted average and FIFO methods.[s] **Ch 9**

    (viii)   Prepare process accounts in situations where work remains incomplete.[s] **Ch 9**

    (ix)   Prepare process accounts where losses and gains are identified at different stages of the process.[s] **Ch 9**

    (x)   Distinguish between by-products and joint products.[k] **Ch 9**

    (xi)   Value by-products and joint products at the point of separation.[s] **Ch 9**

    (xii)   Prepare process accounts in situations where by-products and/or joint products occur.[s] **Ch 9**

(c)   Service/operation costing

    (i)   Identify situations where the use of service/operation costing is appropriate.[k] **Ch 10**

    (ii)   Illustrate suitable unit cost measures that may be used in different service/operation situations.[s] **Ch 10**

    (iii)   Carry out service cost analysis in simple service industry situations.[s] **Ch 10**

(4)   Alternative costing principles

(a)   Explain activity based costing (ABC), target costing, life cycle costing and total quality management (TQM) as alternative cost management techniques.[k] **Ch 11**

(b)   Differentiate ABC, target costing and life cycle costing from the traditional costing techniques (note: calculations are not required).[k] **Ch 11**

C   BUDGETING

(1)   Nature and purpose of budgeting

(a)   Explain why organisations use budgeting.[k] **Ch 13**

(b)   Describe the planning and control cycle in an organisation. [k] **Ch 13**

(c)   Explain the administrative procedures used in the budgeting process.[k] **Ch 13**

(d)   Describe the stages in the budgeting process (including sources of relevant data, planning and agreeing draft budgets and purpose of forecasting and how they link to budgeting).[k] **Ch 13**

(2)   Statistical techniques

(a)   Explain the advantages and disadvantages of using high low method to estimate the fixed and variable element of costing.[k] **Ch 4**

(b)   Construct scatter diagrams and lines of best fit.[s] **Ch 3**

(c) Analysis of cost data.

   (i) Explain the concept of correlation coefficient and coefficient of determination.[k] **Ch 12**

   (ii) Calculate and interpret correlation coefficient and coefficient of determination.[s] **Ch 12**

   (iii) Establish a linear function using regression analysis and interpret the results.[s] **Ch 12**

(d) Use liner regression coefficients to make forecasts of costs and revenues.[s] **Ch 12**

(e) Adjust historical and forecast data for price movements.[s] **Ch 12**

(f) Explain the advantages and disadvantages of linear regression analysis.[k] **Ch 12**

(g) Describe the product life cycle and explain its importance in forecasting.[k] **Ch 12**

(h) Explain the principles of time series analysis (cyclical, trend, seasonal variation and random elements).[k] **Ch 12**

(i) Calculate moving averages.[s] **Ch 12**

(j) Calculation of trend, including the use of regression coefficients.[s] **Ch 12**

(k) Use trend and seasonal variation (additive and multiplicative) to make budget forecasts.[s] **Ch 12**

(l) Explain the advantages and disadvantages of time series analysis.[k] **Ch 12**

(m) Explain the purpose of index numbers.[k] **Ch 12**

(n) Calculate simple index numbers for one or more variables. [s] **Ch 12**

(o) Explain the role and features of a computer spreadsheet system.[k] **Ch 18**

(p) Identify applications for computer spreadsheets and their use in cost and management accounting.[s] **Ch 18**

(3) Budget preparation

(a) Explain the importance of principal budget factor in constructing the budget.[k] **Ch 13**

(b) Prepare sales budgets.[s] **Ch 13**

(c) Prepare functional budgets (production, raw materials usage and purchases, labour, variable and fixed overheads).[s] **Ch 13**

(d) Prepare cash budgets.[s] **Ch 13**

(e) Prepare master budgets (income statement and statement of financial position).[s] **Ch 13**

(f) Explain and illustrate 'what if' analysis and scenario planning.[s] **Ch 13**

(4) Flexible budgets

(a) Explain the importance of flexible budgets in control.[k] **Ch 13**

(b) Explain the disadvantage of fixed budgets in control.[k] **Ch 13**

(c) Identify situations where fixed or flexible budgetary control would be appropriate.[k] **Ch 13**

(d) Flex a budget to a given level of volume.[s] **Ch 13**

(5) Capital budgeting and discounted cash flows

(a) Discuss the importance of capital investment and planning and control.[k] **Ch 14**

(b) Define and distinguish between capital and revenue expenditure.[k] **Ch 14**

(c) Outline the issues to consider and the steps involved in the preparation of a capital expenditure budget.[k] **Ch 14**

(d) Explain and illustrate the difference between simple and compound interest, and between nominal and effective interest rates.[s] **Ch 14**

(e) Explain and illustrate compounding and discounting.[s] **Ch 14**

(f) Explain the distinction between cash flow and profit and the relevance of cash flow to capital investment appraisal.[k] **Ch 14**

(g) Identify and evaluate relevant cash flows for individual investment decisions.[s] **Ch 14**

(h) Explain and illustrate the net present value (NPV) and internal rate of return (IRR) methods of discounted cash flow.[s] **Ch 14**

(i) Calculate present value using annuity and perpetuity formulae.[s] **Ch 14**

(j) Calculate NPV, IRR and payback (discounted and non-discounted).[s] **Ch 14**

(k) Interpret the results of NPV, IRR and payback calculations of investment viability.[s] **Ch 14**

(6) Budgetary control and reporting

(a) Calculate simple variances between flexed budget, fixed budget and actual sales, costs and profits.[s] **Ch 13**

(b) Discuss the relative significance of variances.[k] **Ch 15**

(c) Explain potential action to eliminate variances.[k] **Ch 15**

(d) Define the concept of responsibility accounting and its significance in control.[k] **Ch 13**

(e) Explain the concept of controllable and uncontrollable costs.[k] **Ch 13**

(f) Prepare control reports suitable for presentation to management (to include recommendation of appropriate control action).[s] **Ch 13**

(7) Behavioural aspects of budgeting

(a) Explain the importance of motivation in performance management.[k] **Ch 13**

(b) Identify factors in a budgetary planning and control system that influence motivation.[k] **Ch 13**

(c) Explain the impact of targets upon motivation.[k] **Ch 13**

(d) Discuss managerial incentive schemes.[k] **Ch 13**

(e) Discuss the advantages and disadvantages of a participative approach to budgeting.[k] **Ch 13**

(f) Explain top down, bottom up approaches to budgeting.[k] **Ch 13**

D STANDARD COSTING

(1) Standard costing systems

(a) Explain the purpose and principles of standard costing.[k] **Ch 15**

(b) Explain the difference between standard, marginal and absorption costing.[k] **Ch 15**

(c)   Establish the standard cost per unit under absorption and marginal costing.[k] **Ch 15**

(2)   Variance calculations and analysis

(a)   Calculate sales price and volume variance.[s] **Ch 15**

(b)   Calculate materials total, price and usage variance.[s] **Ch 15**

(c)   Calculate labour total, rate and efficiency variance.[s] **Ch 15**

(d)   Calculate variable overhead total, expenditure and efficiency.[s] **Ch 15**

(e)   Calculate fixed overhead total, expenditure and, where appropriate, volume, capacity and efficiency.[s] **Ch 15**

(f)   Interpret the variances.[s] **Ch 15**

(g)   Explain factors to consider before investigating variances, explain possible causes of the variances and recommend control action.[s] **Ch 15**

(h)   Explain the interrelationships between the variances.[k] **Ch 15**

(i)   Calculate actual or standard figures where the variances are given.[k] **Ch 15**

(3)   Reconciliation of budgeted profit and actual profit

(a)   Reconcile budgeted profit with actual profit under standard absorption costing.[s] **Ch 15**

(b)   Reconcile budgeted profit or contribution with actual profit or contribution under standard marginal costing.[s] **Ch 15**

E   PERFORMANCE MEASUREMENT

(1)   Performance measurement overview

(a)   Discuss the purpose of mission statements and their role in performance measurement.[k] **Ch 1**

(b)   Discuss the purpose of strategic and operational and tactical objectives and their role in performance measurement.[k] **Ch 16**

(c)   Discuss the impact of economic and market condition on performance measurement.[k] **Ch 16**

(d)   Explain the impact of government regulation on performance measurement.[k] **Ch 16**

(2)   Performance measurement – application

(a)   Discuss and calculate measures of financial performance (profitability, liquidity, activity and gearing) and non- financial measures.[s] **Ch 16**

(b)   Perspectives of the balance scorecard.

    (i)   Discuss the advantages and limitations of the balance scorecard.[k] **Ch 16**

    (ii)   Describe performance indicators for financial success, customer satisfaction, process efficiency and growth.[k] **Ch 16**

    (iii)   Discuss critical success factors and key performance indicators and their link to objectives and mission statements.[k] **Ch 16**

    (iv)   Establish critical success factors and key performance indicators in a specific situation.[s] **Ch 16**

(c)   Economy, efficiency and effectiveness

    (i)   Explain the concepts of economy, efficiency and effectiveness.[k] **Ch 17**

    (ii)   Describe performance indicators for economy, efficiency and effectiveness.[k] **Ch 17**

     (iii)   Establish performance indicators for economy, efficient and effectiveness in a specific situation.[s] **Ch 17**

     (iv)   Discuss the meaning of each of the efficiency, capacity and activity ratios.[k] **Ch 16**

     (v)   Calculate the efficiency, capacity and activity ratios in a specific situation.[s] **Ch 16**

(d)   Unit costs

     (i)   Describe performance measures which would be suitable in contract and process costing environments.[k] **Ch 17**

(e)   Resources utilisation

     (i)   Describe measures of performance utilisation in service and manufacturing environments.[k] **Ch 16**

     (ii)   Establish measures of resource utilisation in a specific situation.[s] **Ch 16**

(f)   Profitability

     (i)   Calculate return on investment and residual income.[s] **Ch 17**

     (ii)   Explain the advantages and limitations of return on investment and residual income.[k] **Ch 17**

(g)   Quality of service

     (i)   Distinguish performance measurement issues in service and manufacturing industries.[k] 1 **Ch 16/17**

     (ii)   Describe performance measures appropriate for service industries.[k] **Ch 17**

(3)   **Cost reductions and value enhancement**

(a)   Compare cost control and cost reduction.[s] **Ch 17**

(b)   Describe and evaluate cost reduction methods.[s] **Ch 17**

(c)   Describe and evaluate value analysis.[s] **Ch 17**

(4)   **Monitoring performance and reporting**

(a)   Discuss the importance of non-financial performance measures.[k] **Ch 16**

(b)   Discuss the relationship between short-term and long-term performance.[k] **Ch 16**

(c)   Discuss the measurement of performance in service industry situations.[k] **Ch 17**

(d)   Discuss the measurement of performance in non-profit seeking and public sector organisations.[k] **Ch 17**

(e)   Discuss measures that may be used to assess managerial performance and the practical problems involved.[k] **Ch 17**

(f)   Discuss the role of benchmarking in performance measurement.[k] **Ch 16**

(g)   Produce reports highlighting key areas for management attention and recommendations for improvement.[k] **Ch 17**

TOP 10 TIPS TO IMPROVE YOUR RESULT

Be organised and plan your study time – there are more tips on how to do this below.

'Mens sana in corpore sano' – prepare your body; sleep well and eat right as a healthy body leads to a healthy mind!

Study according to your learning style – different people have different learning styles. Some people are visual learners, some people prefer sound, some need physical motion – try out different methods to see what works best for you.

Try using a study buddy – this could be someone taking the same exam, or a friend or family member.

Revise knowledge efficiently – stay focused, stop procrastinating and don't let your mind wander.

Read questions very carefully – many students fail to answer the actual question set. Read the question once right through and then again more slowly. Make note of key words in the question when you read through it.

Ensure you know the structure of the exam – how many questions (and of what type) you will be expected to answer. During your revision, attempt all the different styles of questions you may be asked.

Be a good test-taker. Get lots of practice – the ACCA release sample assessments and practice CBE mock exams are available.

Read good newspapers and professional journals, especially ACCA's *Student Accountant* – this can give you a distinct advantage in the exam.

Adopt a positive mental attitude. You may have nerves and feel anxious but with the correct preparation and practice you can have confidence in your ability to succeed.

PLAN YOUR STUDY TIME

Decide which times of the week you will devote to revising.

Put the times you plan to revise onto a study plan for the weeks from now until the exam and set yourself targets for each period of revision, ensuring that you cover the whole syllabus.

If you are studying for more than one paper at a time, try to mix and match your subjects as this can help you to keep motivated and see each subject in its broader context.

When working through your course, compare your progress with your plan and, if you fall behind, re-plan your work (perhaps including extra sessions). If you are ahead, do some extra revision/practice questions.

EXTRA QUESTIONS

Practising exam standard questions is a critical part of your revision.

Specimen Exams and Practice Tests are available from
http://www.accaglobal.com/gb/en/student/exam-support-resources.html

and Exam Kits and Mock Exams in the style of the real exam can be obtained from

http://kaplan-publishing.kaplan.co.uk/acca-books/pages/acca-books.aspx.

1 Accounting for management

The following topics are covered in this chapter:
- The nature of good information
- The managerial processes of planning, decision making and control
- Mission statements
- Levels of planning
- Responsibility accounting
- Financial, cost and management accounting

1.1 THE NATURE OF GOOD INFORMATION

LEARNING SUMMARY

After studying this section you should be able to:

- distinguish between data and information
- identify and explain the attributes of good information.

Data and information

DEFINITION **Data** consists of numbers, letters, symbols, raw facts, events and transactions which have been recorded but not yet processed into a form suitable for use.

Data and information are terms which need to be distinguished. Although some may use these terms interchangeably they have distinct differences.

DEFINITION **Information** is data that has been processed in such a way that someone can use it in order to make decisions.

Attributes of good information

Management use information to be able to plan, control and make decisions. A high quality of information improves management's decision making. Good information has to be:

Note the three managerial processes that are identified.

Accurate	The degree of accuracy depends on the reason why the information is needed.
Complete	Information should be sufficient and not excessive.
Cost effective	The value of information should exceed the cost of producing it.
Understandable	Use of technical language or jargon must be limited.
Relevant	The information should be relevant to its purpose.
Accessible	Information should be accessible via the appropriate channels of communication to the appropriate persons.
Timely	Information should be provided to a manager in time for decisions to be made based on that information.
Easy to use	Information should be easy to use for the purposes intended.

1.2 THE MANAGERIAL PROCESSES OF PLANNING, DECISION MAKING AND CONTROL

LEARNING SUMMARY

After studying this section you should be able to:

- outline the managerial processes of planning, decision making and control.

Managerial processes

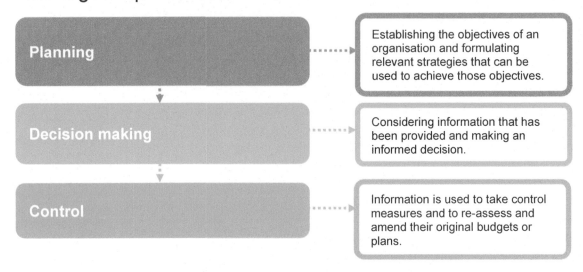

Planning	Establishing the objectives of an organisation and formulating relevant strategies that can be used to achieve those objectives.
Decision making	Considering information that has been provided and making an informed decision.
Control	Information is used to take control measures and to re-assess and amend their original budgets or plans.

KEY POINT The processes are connected as the first part of the decision-making process is planning, the second part is control.

1.3 MISSION STATEMENTS

LEARNING SUMMARY

After studying this section you should be able to:

- outline the use and content of a mission statement.

The mission of the business needs to be established before planning can take place.

KEY POINT The mission statement is a statement in writing that describes the overall aims and purpose of an organisation.

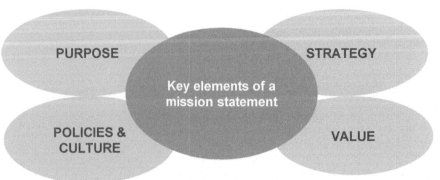

PURPOSE

STRATEGY

Key elements of a mission statement

POLICIES & CULTURE

VALUE

Purpose	Why does the business exist?
Strategy	What does the business provide and how is it provided?
Policies & culture	How does the business expect its staff to act/behave?
Value	What are the core principles of the business?

Research the mission statements of different businesses to see how the elements are addressed.

Mission statements will have some or all of the following characteristics:

- Usually a brief statement of no more than a page in length
- A very general statement of entity culture
- A statement of the aims of the organisation
- A statement of the intended business areas to operate
- Open-ended (not in quantifiable terms)
- Not inclusive of commercial terms, such as desired profit
- Not time-assigned
- Forms a basis of communication to the people inside the organisation and to people outside the organisation
- Used to formulate goal statements, objectives and short term targets
- Guides the direction of the entity's strategy

1.4 LEVELS OF PLANNING

LEARNING SUMMARY

After studying this section you should be able to:

- define the use of SMART when generating aims and objectives
- explain the difference between strategic, tactical and operational planning.

KEY POINT Aims and objectives generated based upon the mission statement should be SMART.

Specific	Well defined and understandable objectives.
Measurable	Completion of objectives measurable.
Attainable	Resources and skills available for objectives to be achieved.
Relevant	Objectives are relevant for those involved and to the mission of the business.
Timely	Timing of the completion of objectives is achievable and reviews are performed regularly.

There are three levels of planning known as 'planning horizons'. The three levels differ according to the seniority of management involved and their time span.

The planning horizons

Strategic planning and control (LONG TERM)	Senior managers formulate long-term goals and plans for an organisation as a whole linked to achieving the company's mission.
Tactical planning and control (SHORT TERM)	Shorter term plans for individual areas of the business – breaking strategic plans into manageable chunks.
Operational planning and control (DAY TO DAY)	Making day-to-day decisions.

1.5   RESPONSIBILITY ACCOUNTING

LEARNING SUMMARY

After studying this section you should be able to:

- distinguish between cost, profit, investment and revenue centres.

DEFINITION   Responsibility accounting is based on identifying individual parts of a business which are the responsibility of a single manager.

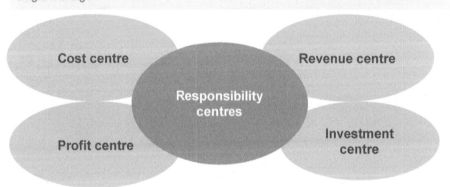

- **Cost centre** – a production or service location, function, activity or item of equipment whose costs are identified and recorded.

- **Revenue centre** – part of the business that earns sales revenue. It is similar to a cost centre, but only revenues, and not costs, are recorded.

- **Profit centre** – part of the business for which both the costs incurred and the revenues earned are identified.

- **Investment centre** – managers of investment centres are responsible for investment decisions as well as decisions affecting costs and revenues.

1.6 FINANCIAL, COST AND MANAGEMENT ACCOUNTING

LEARNING SUMMARY

After studying this section you should be able to:

- describe the purpose and role of cost and management accounting within an organisation

- compare and contrast financial accounting with cost and management accounting

- Identify the limitations in management information.

DEFINITION **Financial accounting** involves preparing financial statements for external users summarising the financial performance for a period of time and the financial position as at a particular date, used for analysis and interpretation.

DEFINITION Cost accounting is a system for recording data and producing information about costs for the products produced by an organisation and/or the services it provides.

> Management accounting has cost accounting as its essential foundation.

DEFINITION Management accounting is the sourcing, analysis, communication and use of financial and non-financial information for use in the organisation and development of its business.

KEY POINT The importance of non-financial information used in management accounting should not be forgotten.

Management versus financial accounting

Management accounting ┄┄▶
- Internal use
- To aid planning, controlling and decision making
- No legal requirements
- Management decide on appropriate format
- Financial and non-financial information
- Historical and forward looking

Financial accounting ┄┄▶
- External use
- To record the financial performance in a period and the financial position at the end of that period
- Limited companies must produce financial accounts
- Format and content of financial accounts intending to give a true and fair view should follow accounting standards and company law
- Mostly financial
- Mainly a historical record

Limitations of management information

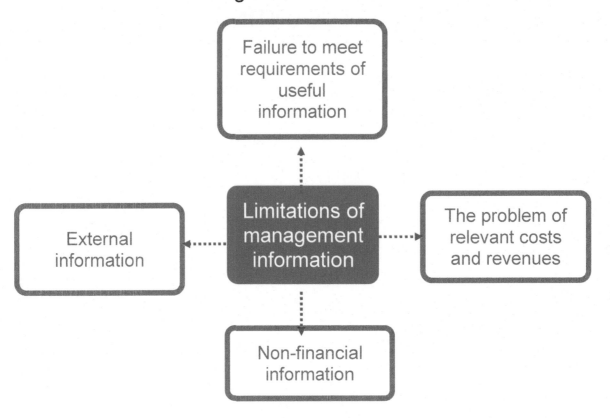

Failure to meet requirements of useful information

If information supplied to managers is deficient in any of the attributes of good information then inappropriate management decisions may be made.

The problem of relevant costs and revenues

Not all information produced by an accounting system is relevant. Information produced mainly for financial reporting purposes and then taken as the basis for management decisions will often need significant modification to be useful to management. Figures presented to assist in management decision-making are those that will be affected by the decision and should be:

> The term 'figures' is referring to costs and revenues.

Future	Costs and revenues incurred in the future rather than 'sunk' costs and revenues of the past.
Incremental	The added extra cost or revenue resulting from taking on a decision.
Cash flows	Actual cash being spent or received.

Non-financial information

Managers will also consider qualitative, behavioural, motivational, even environmental factors.

> Non-financial factors are often difficult to estimate and quantify.

External information

Conventional accounting systems focus entirely on internal information although there are external factors which also need to be considered:

- Government actions
- Competitor actions
- Customer demands
- Other factors such as seasonal changes.

Do you understand?

1 Which of the following relates to management accounts?

    (i)   Prepared yearly

    (ii)   For internal use

    (iii) Contains future information

2 Which of the following relates to financial accounts?

    (i)   Prepared yearly

    (ii)   For internal use

    (iii) Contains future information

3 Strategic planning is carried out by senior managers and is concerned with long-term planning. Both quantitative and qualitative information is used.

True or false?

4 Identify which of the following an investment centre manager is responsible for:

    (i)   costs

    (ii)   revenues

    (iii) expenditure on non-current assets

1 (ii) and (iii) only. Management accounts are for internal use and contain future information.

2 (i) only. Financial accounts are prepared yearly whereas management accounts are prepared on a more timely basis.

3 True

4 (i), (ii), (iii) Investment managers are responsible for revenues, costs and expenditure on non-current assets.

1   **The manager of a profit centre is responsible for which of the following?**

   (i)   Revenues of the centre

   (ii)   Costs of the centre

   (iii) Assets employed in the centre

   A   (i) only

   B   (ii) only

   C   (i) and (ii) only

   D   (i), (ii) and (iii)

2   The following statements relate to financial accounting or to cost and management accounting:

   (i)   Financial accounts are historical records.

   (ii)   Cost accounting is part of financial accounting and establishes costs incurred by an organisation.

   (iii) Management accounting is used to aid planning, control and decision making.

   Which of the statements are correct?

   A   (i) and (ii) only

   B   (i) and (iii) only

   C   (ii) and (iii) only

   D   (i), (ii) and (iii)

3   Emily is the manager of production department A2 in a factory which has five other production departments.

   She receives monthly information that compares planned and actual expenditure for department A2. After department A2, all production goes into other factory departments to be completed prior to being despatched to customers. Decisions involving capital expenditure in department A2 are not taken by Emily.

   Which of the following describes Emily's role in department A2?

   A   A cost centre manager

   B   An investment centre manager

   C   A revenue centre manager

   D   A profit centre manager

2 Sources of data

The following topics are covered in this chapter:

- Types of data
- Internal and external sources of data
- General economic environment
- Sampling techniques

2.1 TYPES OF DATA

Primary and secondary data

DEFINITION **Primary data** is obtained directly from first-hand sources by means of surveys, observation or experimentation.

Information collected for one purpose by a business and then, at a later date, used again for another purpose would no longer be primary data.

DEFINITION **Secondary data** is data that has been collected or researched recently. Sources of secondary data include the internet, libraries, company reports, newspaper, governments and banks.

KEY POINT Primary data is preferable to secondary data.

Problems of using secondary data

Data quickly becomes out of date.

The data may be incomplete.

As the data was sourced by someone else, there is no control over how it was sourced.

Problems of using secondary data

Is it actual data, seasonally adjusted, estimated or a projection?

The original reason for collecting the data may be unknown.

Users must be aware of the limitations of making decisions based on information produced from secondary data.

Discrete and indiscrete data

DEFINITION Discrete data is data that can only take certain values. It can be numerical and categorical. For example the number of CD sales, a CD cannot be split up – there is nothing between one CD or two CDs.

DEFINITION Continuous data is data that is not restricted to defined separate values. It can occupy any value over a continuous range.

2.2 INTERNAL AND EXTERNAL SOURCES OF DATA

LEARNING SUMMARY

After studying this section you should be able to:

- identify internal and external data sources and their benefits and limitations.

| INTERNAL DATA SOURCES | ┈┈▶ | Internal information may come from various sources:
• the accounting system
• the payroll system
• the strategic planning system. |

| EXTERNAL DATA SOURCES | ┈┈▶ | External information may come from various sources:
• government sources
• customers and suppliers
• trade associations and trade journals
• media including the financial and business press
• the internet. |

Benefits and limitations of internal data sources

Benefits	Limitations
Data can easily be sorted and analysed.	
Readily available data.	Further analysis may be required to make the data useful for management use.
Reports can easily be produced when required.	
Data relates directly to the organisation concerned.	

Benefits and limitations of external data sources

Benefits	Limitations
Wide expanse of external sources of information.	Finding relevant information can be time consuming.
Easily accessible especially using the internet.	
More general information available.	Data may contain inaccuracies.
Can source specific information needs.	

2.3 GENERAL ECONOMIC ENVIRONMENT

LEARNING SUMMARY

After studying this section you should be able to:

* understand how the general economic environment impacts a business both nationally and internationally.

The impact of changing interest rates, exchange rates, inflation and general economic activity will impact on the productivity and profitability of businesses

Interest rates	Interest rates affect the cost of borrowing money. If interest rates rise this impacts the cost of borrowing i.e. loans and bank overdrafts. It will also impact the spending habits of consumers who will also have increased borrowing costs to meet.
Inflation	Inflation is a sustained increase in the general level of prices for goods and services. Each unit of currency will be able to purchase fewer goods and services.
Exchange rates	An exchange rate is expressed in terms of the quantity of one currency that can be exchanged for one unit of the other currency. If exchange rates change, businesses are more open to risk in relation to receivable and payable balances, revision of prices and investments overseas being uncertain.

KEY POINT Businesses need to consider the general economic state and how it is forecast to change when forecasting productivity and pricing strategies.

2.4 SAMPLING TECHNIQUES

After studying this section you should be able to:

- define a population and a sample
- understand why sampling is necessary
- explain sampling techniques (random, systematic, stratified, multi-stage, cluster and quota).

DEFINITION Population is all the items under consideration in a particular enquiry.

DEFINITION A **sample** is a group of items drawn from that population.

KEY POINT The purpose of sampling is to gain as much information as possible about the population by observing only a small proportion of that population.

The whole population may not be known.

It may be too costly to test every item in a population.

Why is sampling necessary?

Testing data may damage or destroy data.

The sample must be of a certain size – the larger the size the more reliable the results. The sample must be chosen in a way that is representative of the population.

Sampling techniques

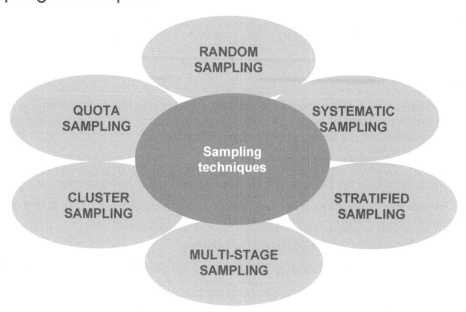

Random sampling	A sample taken so every member of the population has an equal chance of being selected. This can be achieved by numbering each item in the population.
Systematic sampling	Also known as 'quasi-random'. Sample members are selected according to a random starting point and a fixed periodic interval.
Stratified sampling	The population is divided into separate groups, called 'strata'. A random sample is then drawn from each group.
Cluster sampling	The population is divided into separate groups called 'clusters'. A simple random sample of clusters is then selected from the population.
Multi-stage sampling	A method which is applied for large populations, multi stage sampling can be a more complex form of cluster sampling. The population is divided into groups (or clusters) then one or more groups are chosen at random and then everyone within the chosen group is sampled.
Quota sampling	A tailored sample in proportion to a characteristic or trait of a population.

Do you understand?

1   A sample is taken by dividing the population into different age bands and then sampling randomly from the bands, in proportion to their size. What is such a sample called; simple random, stratified random, quota or cluster?

2   The essence of systematic sampling is that:

    A   each element of the population has an equal chance of being chosen

    B   members of various strata are selected by the interviewers up to predetermined limits

    C   every nth member of the population is selected

    D   every element of one definable subsection of the population is selected

3   Associate with each of the following sampling methods A – F the most appropriate example from the list 1– 6, given below.

    A   Simple random sample

    B   Stratified random sample

    C   Cluster sample

    D   Systematic sample

    E   Quota sample

    F   Multistage sample

Examples

    (1)   One city is chosen at random from all cities in the United Kingdom, then the electoral register is used to select a 1-per-1,000 sample.

    (2)   Names picked from a hat.

    (3)   Every 10th person is chosen randomly from each ward in a hospital.

    (4)   One secondary school in a town is selected at random, then every pupil in that school is surveyed.

    (5)   One person in ten is chosen from an alphabetical list of employees.

    (6)   People are stopped in the street according to instructions such as 'stop equal numbers of men and women'.

3   A2 B3 C4 D5 E6 F1

2   C In systematic sampling, population members are listed and members selected at regular intervals along the list.

1   Stratified random sampling. In simple random sampling, there is no division of the population into groups. In cluster sampling, only one group is selected and all its members are surveyed. Quota sampling and stratified random sampling are both as described in the question but quota sampling is not random.

14

1   A firm which bottles shampoo selects some filled bottles for examination. The procedure used is to select a random starting point x (xth bottle filled) and every bottle at an interval of y is then chosen for examination.

    What is this type of sampling known as?

    A   Multi-stage

    B   Random

    C   Systematic

    D   Stratified

2   The following statements are often made about 'simple random sampling'.

    (i)   It ensures a representative sample.

    (ii) It eliminates selection bias.

    Which of the following is always true?

    A   (i) only

    B   (ii) only

    C   Both (i) and (ii)

    D   Neither (i) nor (ii)

3   **Which of the following describes secondary data?**

    A   data that does not provide any information

    B   data collected for another purpose

    C   data collected specifically for the purpose of the survey being undertaken

    D   data collected by post or telephone, not by personal interview

3 Presenting information

The following topics are covered in this chapter:

- Preparation of reports
- Presenting information using tables, charts and graphs
- Interpreting information

3.1 PREPARATION OF REPORTS

LEARNING SUMMARY

After studying this section you should be able to:

- outline the four stage approach to report writing
- outline the structure of a report
- prepare written reports representing management information in suitable formats according to purpose.

Information is fundamental to management accounting. One of the most desirable qualities of information is that it should be understandable to the user.

The four-stage approach to report writing

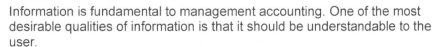

Prepare	Determine the type of document that is required. Establish the user of the information. Understand what the report will be used for.
Plan	Select the relevant data required. Produce a logical order for the material.
Write	Determine the appropriate writing style. Take care of spelling, use of language and arithmetic.
Review	Re-read what you have written. Check the requirements of the report are met. Ensure that the report is complete and clear.

Structure of a report

Title	At the top of your report the title should show; who the report is to, who it is from, the date and a heading.

Introduction	The introduction shows what information was requested, the work completed and where the results and conclusions can be found.

Analysis	The analysis presents the information required in a series of subsections.

| Conclusion | A conclusion provides recommendations. New information should not be introduced to a conclusion. |

| Appendices | Appendices will contain detailed calculations, tables of underlying data, etc. References to appendices should be made in the report, as appropriate. |

3.2 PRESENTING INFORMATION USING TABLES, CHARTS AND GRAPHS

LEARNING SUMMARY

After studying this section you should be able to:

- outline the content and use of tables

- present information using table, charts and graphs.

Tables

DEFINITION   **Tabulation** is the process of presenting data in the form of a table. A **table** is an arrangement of rows and columns which summarises information and presents it in a more understandable way.

A table should be clear and unambiguous, including the following:

Title	Clear and self-explanatory title.
Source	The source of the material used.
Units	Units of measurement e.g. 000s mean that the units are in thousands.
Headings	Column and row headings should be clear and concise.
Totals	Totals and sub-totals shown where appropriate.
Percentages and ratios	Shown if meaningful, with an indication of how they were calculated.

A table is set up in the form of a number of columns headed up across the page and then a number of rows of information moving down the page. An example is given below:

	Column 1	Column 2	Column 3
Row 1			
Row 2			

Graphs and charts

A graph should be clear and unambiguous, including the following:

Title	Clear and self-explanatory.
Source	The source of the material used.
Units	Units of measurement e.g. 000s mean that the units are in thousands.
Scale	Scale for correct interpretation.
Key	Explains contents.
Labelling	Explains what the axes show.

Types of graphs and charts

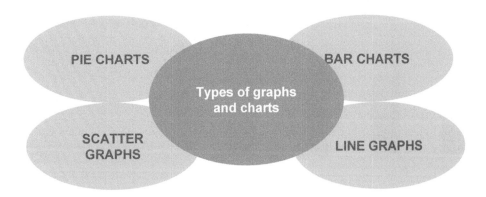

Bar charts

Bar charts are one of the most commonly used types of graph because they are simple to create and very easy to interpret.

There are different types of bar charts, examples of each follow.

- **Simple bar chart** – only one variable is being illustrated.

- **Component bar chart** - shows information about different sub-groups of the main categories.

- **Percentage component bar chart** – shows the data for each category as a percentage of the whole. Each bar is the same height (100%) and each component is represented by a section proportional in size to its representation in the total of each bar.

- **Compound (multiple) bar chart** – shows the same information as a component bar chart but instead of the data being stacked into one column, a separate bar is used for each subgroup.

> Typical scenarios will require the identification of appropriate charts and graphs to use for presenting different data.

Examples of different types of charts

Product sales for business X

Simple bar chart

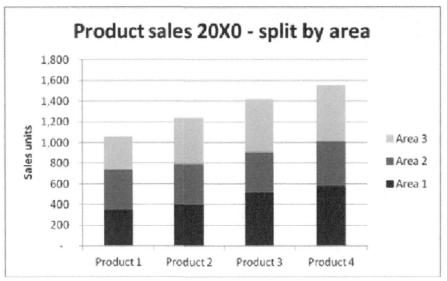

Product sales 20X0 - split by area

Component bar chart

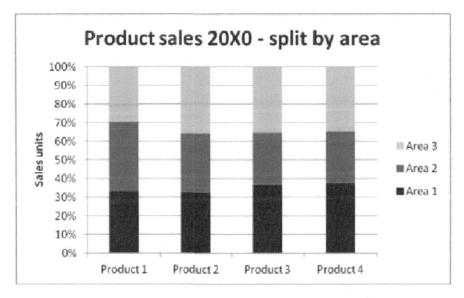

Product sales 20X0 - split by area

Percentage component bar chart

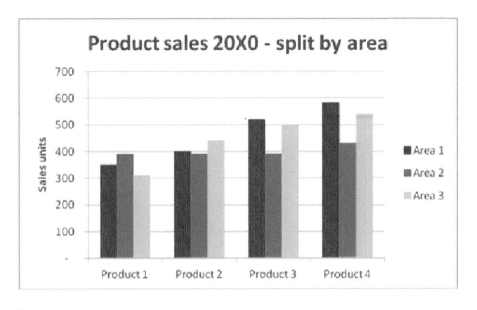

Compound (multiple) bar chart

Line graphs

DEFINITION **Line graphs** are used to show time series data; how one or more variables vary over a continuous period of time.

Scatter diagrams

DEFINITION **Scatter diagrams** are used to show the relationship between pairs of quantitative measurements made for the same object or individual.

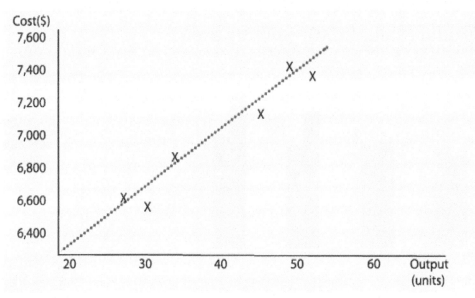

By analysing the pattern of dots that make up a scatter diagram it is possible to identify whether there is any relationship (correlation) between the two measurements. Regression lines, lines of best fit, can also be added to the graph and used to decide whether the relationship between the two sets of measurements can be explained or if it is due to chance.

Pie charts

DEFINITION **A pie chart** is a circular graph that shows the relative contribution that different sub-groups contribute to an overall category. A wedge of the circle represents each sub-groups contribution. Every 1% contribution that a sub-group contributes to the total corresponds to an angle of 3.6 degrees.

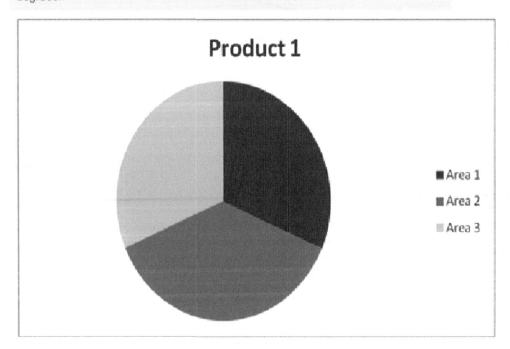

Scenarios may require calculations of the size of the wedges that form the pie chart from data provided.

3.3 INTERPRETING INFORMATION

LEARNING SUMMARY

After studying this section you should be able to:

* interpret information presented in management reports

Although information presented in diagrammatic form should be easy to understand, part of the role of the management accountant may involve interpreting the information, perhaps in the form of a brief report to management.

The objective of interpretation is to bring out the meaning of the information to help management reach conclusions based on the information presented. As a result of the interpretation, suitable recommendations can be made to management.

Take note of the two points raised – establishing the meaning of the information and aiding management in reaching conclusions.

Do you understand?

1   Arlo produces three main products. Which would be the most appropriate chart or diagram for showing total revenue analysed into product revenue month by month?

(i) scatter graph (ii) line graph (iii) pie chart (iv) component bar chart

2   What are the four stages to produce a report?

3   What is the meaning of correlation?

4   What is the objective of interpreting information within management accounting?

1   (iv) A bar chart is a good way of illustrating total sales month by month. The length of the bar each month is a measure of total sales. The bar can be divided into three parts, to show the amount of sales achieved for each of the three products. This is called a component bar chart.
2   The four stage approach includes: preparing, planning, writing and reviewing.
3   Correlation is a mutual relationship or connection between two or more things.
4   The objective of interpretation is to bring out the meaning of the information to help management reach conclusions based on the information presented.

1   The following table shows that the typical salary of part qualified accountants in five different regions of England.

Area	Typical salary
	$
South-east	21,500
Midlands	20,800
North-east	18,200
North-west	17,500
South-west	16,700

Which diagram would be the best one to draw to highlight the differences between areas?

A   a pie diagram

B   a multiple bar chart

C   a percentage component bar chart

D   a simple bar chart

2   A pie chart is being produced to represent the sales from different regional offices of a business:

	$000
North	125
North West	180
East	241
South	691
South East	147
Total	1,384

What would be the angle of the East divisions section on the pie chart (to the nearest whole degree)?

3   **Which member of the sales team had the highest sales in February?**

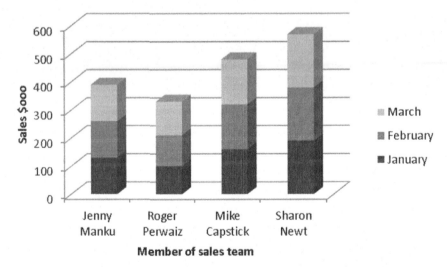

A   Jenny Manku

B   Roger Perwaiz

C   Mike Capstick

D   Sharon Newt

4 Cost classification

The following topics are covered in this chapter:
- Analysing costs
- Classifying costs
- The high-low method
- Cost equations
- Codes within the costing system

4.1 ANALYSING COSTS

LEARNING SUMMARY

After studying this section you should be able to:

- define a cost in terms of the noun and verb
- understand why costs need to be understood
- outline key terms used in costing
- outline the format and content of a cost card.

DEFINITION Cost *(noun)* is the price of an item; *(verb)* is to estimate the price of.

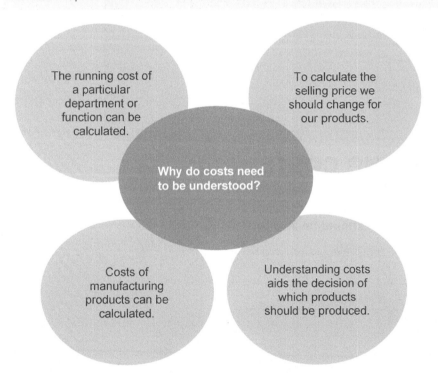

The running cost of a particular department or function can be calculated.

To calculate the selling price we should change for our products.

Why do costs need to be understood?

Costs of manufacturing products can be calculated.

Understanding costs aids the decision of which products should be produced.

Costing terminology

Cost object	A cost object is any activity for which a separate measurement of cost is undertaken.
Cost unit	A cost unit is a unit of product or service in relation to which costs are ascertained.
Cost centre	A cost centre is a production or service location, function, activity or item of equipment for which costs can be ascertained.
Cost card	A cost card is used to show the breakdown of the costs of producing output based on the classification of each cost. A cost card can be produced for one unit or a planned level of production.

These terms are used throughout the syllabus so must be fully understood.

Cost card

The cost card below is an example of a cost card for one unit of product.

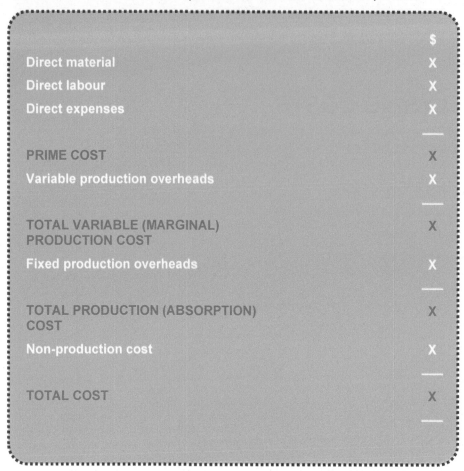

	$
Direct material	X
Direct labour	X
Direct expenses	X
	___
PRIME COST	X
Variable production overheads	X
	___
TOTAL VARIABLE (MARGINAL) PRODUCTION COST	X
Fixed production overheads	X
	___
TOTAL PRODUCTION (ABSORPTION) COST	X
Non-production cost	X
	___
TOTAL COST	X
	___

4.2 CLASSIFYING COSTS

LEARNING SUMMARY

After studying this section you should be able to:

- understand how costs can be classified.

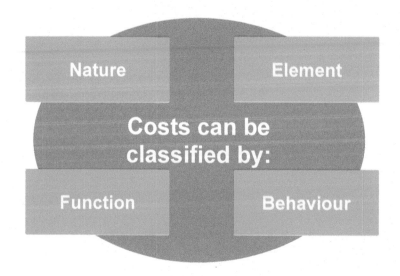

Costs can be classified by: Nature, Element, Function, Behaviour

Classifying cost by element	• **Materials** are the components bought in by the business, used in manufacturing products. • **Labour costs** are the costs of the people working for the organisation. • **Expense costs** are external costs such as rent, business rates, electricity, gas, postage, telephone and similar items.
Classifying cost according to nature	Classified by: • **Direct costs** - clearly identified with the cost object we are trying to cost. • **Indirect costs** - cannot be directly attributed to a particular cost unit, although it is clear that they have been incurred in the production of the product.
Classifying cost according to function	Classified under the functions: • **Production costs** - incurred in the manufacture of the product. • **Non-production costs** - not directly involved in the manufacture of the product, but required to support the overall activity of the business.
Classifying cost by behaviour	Cost behaviour refers to the way in which costs are affected by fluctuations in the level of activity.

Cost behaviours

Costs may be classified according to the way that they behave in relation to changes in levels of activity:

- **Variable costs** – costs that vary in direction proportion with the level of activity. As activity levels increase then total variable costs will also increase.

> Examples of variable costs: direct material, direct labour, variable overheads.

- **Fixed costs** – a cost which is incurred for an accounting period, and which, within certain activity levels, remains constant.

- **Stepped fixed costs** – a type of fixed cost that is only fixed within certain levels of activity. Once the upper limit of an activity level is reached then a new higher level of fixed cost becomes relevant.

- **Semi-variable costs** – contain both fixed and variable cost elements and are therefore partly affected by changes in the level of activity.

Identifying cost behaviours

The behavioural characteristics of costs are used when planning or forecasting costs at different levels of production or activity. When producing a forecast it may be necessary to identify the type of behaviour a cost is exhibiting.

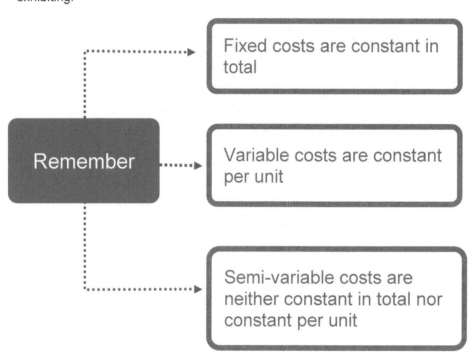

Remember

- Fixed costs are constant in total
- Variable costs are constant per unit
- Semi-variable costs are neither constant in total nor constant per unit

Do you understand?

1 What is a cost card?

2 A cost centre is a production or service location, function, activity or item of equipment for which costs can be ascertained

   True or false?

3 What costs are included in the prime cost?

4 What are the different ways costs can be classified?

1 A cost card is used to show the breakdown of the costs of producing output based on the classification of each cost. A cost card can be produced for one unit or planned level of production.
2 True
3 Prime cost includes; direct materials, direct labour and direct overheads.
4 Costs can be classified by element, nature, function or behaviour.

4.3 THE HIGH-LOW METHOD

LEARNING SUMMARY

After studying this section you should be able to:

- apply the high-low method.

KEY POINT Semi-variable costs need to be split into fixed and variable components.

The high low method picks out the highest and lowest **activity levels** from available data and investigates the change in cost which has occurred between them in order to calculate the variable cost per unit and the fixed cost element.

Step by step approach to the high-low method

Step 1

Select the **highest** and **lowest activity levels**, and their associated costs

Step 2

Calculate the **variable cost (VC) per unit:**

Cost at high level of activity – cost at low level of activity

High level of activity – low level of activity

Step 3

Calculate the **fixed cost by substitution**, using either the high or low activity level:

Total cost at activity level – (Variable cost × Activity level)

Step 4

Use the total fixed cost and the variable cost per unit values from **steps 2 and 3** to calculate the estimated cost at different activity levels.

Total costs = Total fixed costs + (Variable cost per unit × Activity level)

High/low method with stepped fixed costs

It has already been seen that fixed costs can remain fixed only within certain levels of activity. The high/low method can still be used to estimate fixed and variable costs:

Choose the two activity levels where the fixed costs remain unchanged and calculate the variable cost per unit and the total fixed cost using the high/low technique.

Adjustments may need to be made to the fixed costs when calculating the total cost for a new activity level technique.

High/low method with changes in the variable cost per unit

There may be changes in the variable cost per unit, and the high/low method can still be used to determine the fixed and variable elements of semi-variable costs.

> As with the stepped fixed costs – choose activity levels where the variable costs per unit remain unchanged.

4.4 COST EQUATIONS

LEARNING SUMMARY

After studying this section you should be able to:

- outline how cost equations are used for the estimation of future costs.

Cost equations are derived from historical cost data. Once a cost equation has been established, for example distinguishing the fixed and variable costs using the high/low method, it can be used to estimate future costs.

KEY POINT Cost equations are assumed to have a linear function and therefore the equation of a straight line can be applied:

$y = a + bx$

y = dependent variable

x = independent variable

a = intercept on y-axis

b = gradient of the line

Applying the equation to the high/low method:

- 'a' is the fixed cost per period (the intercept)

- 'b' is the variable cost per unit (the gradient)

- 'x' is the activity level (the independent variable

- 'y' is the total cost = fixed cost + variable cost (dependent on the activity level)

4.5 CODES WITHIN THE COSTING SYSTEM

LEARNING SUMMARY

After studying this section you should be able to:

- define a code and outline the different coding methods.

DEFINITION A **code** is a system of symbols designed to be applied to a classified set of items, to give a brief accurate reference, which helps entry into the records, collation and analysis.

Cost codes

When developing a cost code to be used within the costing system, the correct cost centre needs to be decided upon.

- **Generic or functional codes** - Once a cost has been allocated a cost centre code then it may also be useful to know the particular type of expense involved. Digits may be added to the code to represent the precise type of cost.

- **Specific codes** - It may also be necessary for cost allocation, decision making or accounting purposes to allocate a code which specifically identifies the item of cost.

Coding systems

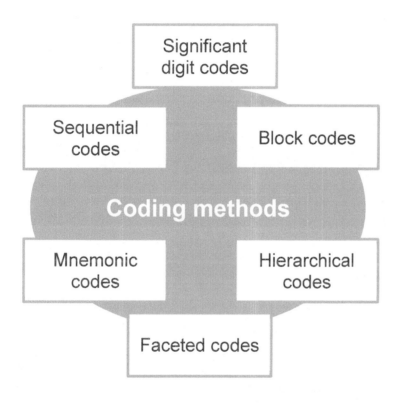

- **Sequential codes** - This is the most basic type of code. It simply means that each code follows a numerical or alphabetical sequence. Planning is needed to determine how many codes might be needed in total.

- **Significant digit codes** - A significant digit code is a code that contains individual digits and letters that are used to represent features of the coded item.

- **Block codes** - Block codes are often used to categorise sequential codes together.

- **Hierarchical codes** - Each digit in the code represents a classification. As the code progresses from left to right each digit represents a smaller subset.

- **Faceted codes** - A faceted code is one that is broken down into a number of facets or fields, each of which signifies a unit of information.

- **Mnemonic codes** - Mnemonic means something that aids the memory or understanding. An alphabetical coding rather than a numerical coding system is used. It is often used to abbreviate or simplify information.

Do you understand?

1   What is the equation of a straight line and how does it apply to the high-low method?

2   Name the 6 different coding methods.

     True or false?

3   What is the purpose of a cost code?

4   What is the first step of the high-low method?

1   The equation of a straight line is y = a + bx. 'a' is the fixed cost per period, 'b' is the variable cost per unit, 'x' is the activity level, 'y' is the total cost = fixed cost + variable cost

2   Significant digit codes, block codes, hierarchical codes, faceted codes, mnemonic codes and sequential codes.

3   A cost code is designed to analyse and classify the costs of an organisation in the most appropriate manner for that organisation.

1 Jet plc is a furniture manufacturer.

How would the following costs be classified?

Cost	Fixed	Variable	Semi-variable
Director's salary			
Wood			
Rent of factory			
Phone bill – includes a line rental			
Factory workers wage			

2 The following production and total cost information relates to a single product organisation for the last three months:

Month	Production units	Total cost $
1	1,200	66,600
2	900	58,200
3	1,400	68,200

The variable cost per unit is constant up to a production level of 2,000 units per month but a step up of $6,000 in the monthly total fixed cost occurs when production reaches 1,100 units per month.

What is the total cost for a month when 1,000 units are produced?

A $54,200

B $55,000

C $59,000

D $60,200

3   The total materials cost of a company is such that when total purchases exceed 15,000 units in any period, then all units purchased, including the first 15,000, are invoiced at a lower cost per unit.

Which of the following graphs is consistent with the behaviour of the total materials cost in a period?

A

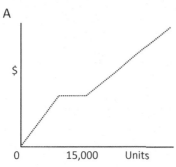

B

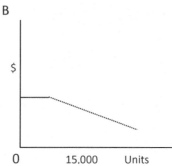

C

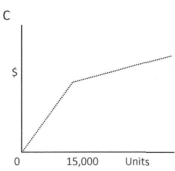

D

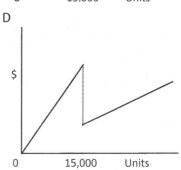

5 Accounting for materials

The following topics are covered in this chapter:

- Inventory control cycle
- Costs of carrying inventory
- Inventory control systems
- Inventory valuation
- The material inventory account

5.1 INVENTORY CONTROL CYCLE

LEARNING SUMMARY

After studying this section you should be able to:

- outline the inventory control cycle in terms of ordering, purchasing and receiving materials.

The procedures for ordering, purchasing and receiving materials are as follows:

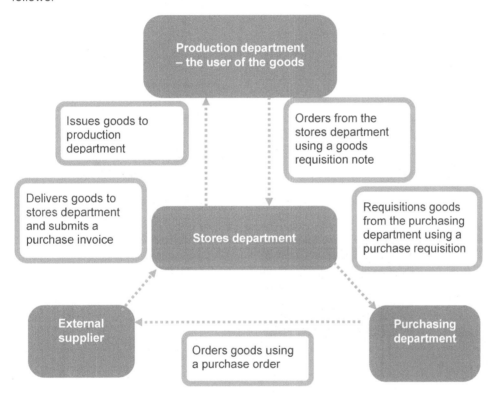

5.2 COSTS OF CARRYING INVENTORY

LEARNING SUMMARY

After studying this section you should be able to:

- understand why inventory is held by a business

- identify the different costs associated with inventory.

KEY POINT Most businesses need to consider which items to have in inventory and how much of each item should be kept.

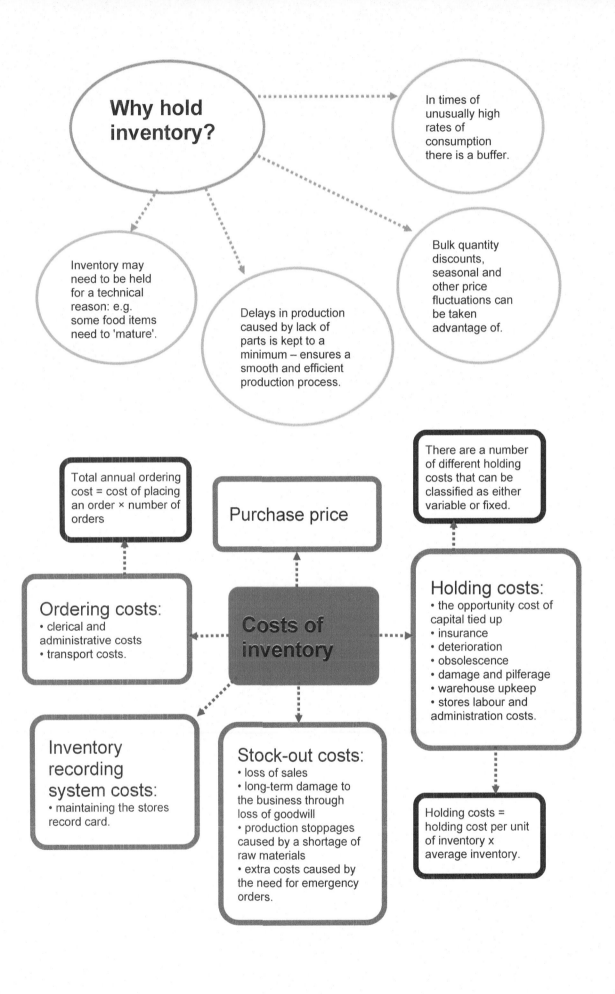

Why hold inventory?

In times of unusually high rates of consumption there is a buffer.

Inventory may need to be held for a technical reason: e.g. some food items need to 'mature'.

Delays in production caused by lack of parts is kept to a minimum – ensures a smooth and efficient production process.

Bulk quantity discounts, seasonal and other price fluctuations can be taken advantage of.

Total annual ordering cost = cost of placing an order × number of orders

Purchase price

There are a number of different holding costs that can be classified as either variable or fixed.

Ordering costs:
• clerical and administrative costs
• transport costs.

Costs of inventory

Holding costs:
• the opportunity cost of capital tied up
• insurance
• deterioration
• obsolescence
• damage and pilferage
• warehouse upkeep
• stores labour and administration costs.

Inventory recording system costs:
• maintaining the stores record card.

Stock-out costs:
• loss of sales
• long-term damage to the business through loss of goodwill
• production stoppages caused by a shortage of raw materials
• extra costs caused by the need for emergency orders.

Holding costs = holding cost per unit of inventory x average inventory.

5.3 INVENTORY CONTROL SYSTEMS

LEARNING SUMMARY

After studying this section you should be able to:

- understand what a re-order level is and how to calculate it

- understand the economic order quantity and how it is calculated

- outline how inventory can be gradually replenished

- identify control procedures to minimise discrepancies and losses.

Re-order level

DEFINITION The **re-order level** is determined with reference to the time it takes to receive an order and the possible inventory requirements during that time.

When the re-order level of inventory is reached a new order must be placed to prevent stock outs.

If the demand in the lead time is constant, the reorder level is calculated as follows:

Re-order level **=** **Maximum usage** **✕** **Maximum lead time**

The economic order quantity (EOQ)

DEFINITION The **EOQ** is the reorder quantity which minimises the total costs associated with holding and ordering inventory (i.e. holding costs + ordering costs).

The EOQ can be estimated graphically by plotting holding costs, ordering costs and total costs at different levels of activity.

KEY POINT The formula to calculate the economic order quantity is:

$$EOQ = \sqrt{\frac{2 \times C_o \times D}{C_h}}$$

C_o = cost of place an order

D = annual demand

C_h – cost of holding one unit of inventory for one year

> The EOQ formula is provided in the exam. However, you should ensure you understand the different symbols and what they represent to use the formula correctly.

There are a number of important assumptions and formulae related to the EOQ:

- Demand and lead time are constant and known

- Purchase price is constant

- No buffer inventory is held.

The economic order quantity (EOQ) with discounts

If a quantity discount is accepted this will have the following effects:

- the annual purchase price will decrease
- the annual holding cost will increase
- the annual ordering cost will decrease.

Steps to calculate the EOQ when quantity discounts are available

1	Calculate the EOQ, ignoring discounts.
2	If the EOQ is smaller than the minimum purchase quantity to obtain a bulk discount, calculate the total for the EOQ of the annual inventory holding costs, inventory ordering costs and inventory purchase costs.
3	Recalculate the annual inventory holding costs, inventory ordering costs and inventory purchase costs for a purchase order size that is only just large enough to qualify for the bulk discount.
4	Compare the total costs when the order quantity is the EOQ with the total costs when the order quantity is just large enough to obtain the discount. Select the minimum cost alternative.
5	If there is a further discount available for an even larger order size, repeat the same calculations for the higher discount level.

Gradual replenishment of inventory

Organisations who replenish inventory levels gradually by manufacturing their own products internally also need to calculate the most economical batch size to produce:

The amended EOQ model is known as the Economic Batch Quantity (EBQ) model.

> There are two choices: produce large batches at long intervals or produce small batches at short intervals

DEFINITION The **EBQ** model is primarily concerned with determining the number of items that should be produced in a batch (compared to the size of an order with the EOQ).

KEY POINT The formula to calculate the economic batch quantity is:

$$EOQ = \sqrt{\frac{2C_o\,D}{C_h\left(1 - \frac{D}{R}\right)}}$$

Q = Batch size

D = Demand per annum

C_h = Cost of holding one unit for one year

C_o = Cost of setting up one batch ready to be produced

R = = Annual replenishment rate

> The EBQ formula is provided in the exam. However, you should ensure you understand the different symbols and what they represent to use the formula correctly.

Control procedures to minimise losses and discrepancies

Stocktaking is checking the physical quantity of inventory held on a certain date and then checking this balance against the balances on the stores ledger (record) cards or bin cards. Stocktaking can be carried out on a periodic basis or a continuous basis.

Other issues and control measures are outlined:

Control measure	Issue avoided
Use of standard costs for purchases. Quotation for special items.	Ordering goods at inflated prices.
Separation of ordering and purchasing. Physical controls over materials receipts, usage and inventory.	Fictitious purchases.
Checking in all goods inwards at gate. Delivery signatures.	Shortages on receipts.
Regular stocktaking. Physical security procedures.	Losses from inventor.
Control of responsible official over all write-offs.	Writing off obsolete or damaged inventory which is good.
Records of all issues. Standard usage allowance.	Losses after issue to production.

5.4   INVENTORY VALUATION

LEARNING SUMMARY

After studying this section you should be able to:

- outline the different methods (FIFO, LIFO and AVCO) of valuing the internal issues from stores to production

- identify the advantages and disadvantages of each method.

The cost of materials is normally derived from suppliers' invoices with the value of internal issues from stores to the user (production) department requiring calculation. The methods that can be used to calculate the value of internal issues are addressed in this section.

DEFINITION   Perpetual inventory is the recording as they occur of receipts, issues and the resulting balances of individual items of inventory in either quantity or quantity and value.

Inventory records are updated using stores ledger cards and bin cards. Bin cards also show a record of receipts, issues and balances of the quantity of an item of inventory handled by stores. As with the stores ledger card, bin cards will show materials received (from purchases and returns) and issued (from requisitions).

Tasks may require the application of a method of valuing internal issues – ensure you are comfortable with how FIFO, LIFO and AVCO are applied.

A basic stores ledger card is shown:

Date	Receipts			Issues			Balance	
	Qty	Per unit	Value	Qty	Per unit	Value	Qty	Value

The value of the issues will depend on whether FIFO, LIFO or AVCO is being used.

First in, first out (FIFO)

DEFINITION FIFO (First in, first out) – assumes that issues will be made based on the oldest prices leaving the more recent prices in stores. FIFO is acceptable by HMRC and adheres to IAS2 Inventories.

Advantages	Disadvantages
Logical – reflects the most likely physical flow..	Less up to date prices are used to value issues to production.
Provides an up to date closing inventory valuation as more recent prices remain in inventory at the period end.	Using FIFO may cause identical jobs to have different costs associated to them.
Acceptable to HM Revenue and Customs and IAS2.	

Last in, first out (LIFO)

DEFINITION LIFO (Last in, first out) – assumes that issues will be made based on the newest prices leaving the oldest prices in stores. LIFO should only be used within an organisation as it does not adhere to IAS2.

Consideration must also be given to how the different methods will impact profit. To do this you must be made aware of whether prices are rising or falling over time.

Advantages	Disadvantages
	Less up to date prices are used to value closing inventory.
Provides an up to date valuation for issues as more recent prices are used to value issues to production.	Not usually acceptable to HM Revenue & Customs and the accounting standards.

Average weighted cost

DEFINITION AVCO (weighted average) – assumes that issues will be made based on the average cost per unit of the items in stores.

Advantages	Disadvantages
AVCO is a compromise on inventory valuation. It is logical as all units have the same value.	An average price rarely reflects the actual purchase price.
Acceptable to the accounting standards and HM Revenue & Customs.	

KEY POINT The formula to calculate the weighted average price is:

Weighted average price = <u>Running total of costs</u>
Running total of units

5.5 THE MATERIAL INVENTORY ACCOUNT

LEARNING SUMMARY

After studying this section you should be able to:

- outline the entries made to the material inventory account.

Materials held in store are an asset recorded as inventory in the statement of financial position, relating transactions are recorded in the material inventory account.

Entries to the material inventory account are as shown:

Debit	Credit
Increase inventory for:	Decrease inventory for:
Purchases	Issues to production
Returns to stores	Returns to suppliers

Do you understand?

1   How can the issue of ordering goods at inflated prices be prevented?

(i) Use of standard costs (ii) Regular stocktaking (iii) Checking in all goods inwards

2   LIFO assumes that issues will be made based on the oldest prices leaving the more recent prices in stores.

True or false?

3   If items of inventory have been returned to the stores department will this be debited or credited to the material inventory account?

4   How is the weighted average price calculated?

1   (i)
2   False it is FIFO that assumes issues will be made based on the oldest prices leaving the more recent prices in stores.
3   Returns back to the stores department will be debited to the material inventory account as the balance of inventory is increasing.
4   Weighted average price = <u>Running total of costs</u>
Running total of units

1 A manufacturing company uses 28,000 components at an even rate during the year. Each order placed with the supplier of the components is for 1,500 components, which is the economic order quantity. The company holds a buffer inventory of 700 components. The annual cost of holding one component in inventory is $3.

What is the total annual cost of holding inventory of the component?

$

2 In the year ended 31 August 20X4, Aplus' records show closing inventory of 1,000 units compared to 950 units of opening inventory.

Which of the following statements is true assuming that prices have fallen throughout the year?

A   Closing inventory and profit are higher using FIFO rather than AVCO

B   Closing inventory and profit are lower using FIFO rather than AVCO

C   Closing inventory is higher and profit lower using FIFO rather than AVCO

D   Closing inventory is lower and profit higher using FIFO rather than AVCO

3 Inventory movements for product X during the last quarter were as follows:

January	Purchases	10 items at $19.80 each
February	Sales	10 items at $30 each
March	Purchases	20 items at $24.50
	Sales	5 items at $30 each

Opening inventory at 1 January was 6 items valued at $15 each.

What would the gross profit be for the quarter using the weighted average cost method?

A $135.75

B $155.00

C $174.00

D $483.00

Accounting for labour

The following topics are covered in this chapter:

- Remuneration methods
- Direct and indirect labour
- Labour costs in the accounting system
- Labour ratios

6.1 REMUNERATION METHODS

LEARNING SUMMARY

After studying this section you should be able to:

- describe different remuneration methods: time-based systems and piecework systems.

Time-related systems

The most common remuneration method is to calculate pay or wages on the number of hours an employee works. Employees are paid a basic rate per hour, day, week or month.

- **Time-based systems** do not on the whole provide any incentive for employees to improve productivity and close supervision is often necessary.

- **Overtime** can be paid if any extra hours are worked.

- A **guaranteed minimum wage** is often required due to minimum wage requirements.

> You should be able to calculate amounts of pay based on information provided whether that is for a time-related or output-related system.

KEY POINT Total wages = (total hours worked × basic rate of pay per hour) + (overtime hours worked × overtime premium per hour).

Output-related systems

A piecework system pays a fixed amount per unit produced.

KEY POINT Total wages = (units produced × rate of pay per unit)

- **Piecework** is often combined with a time-based system to provide an added incentive to employees.

- A **guaranteed minimum wage** is often required due to minimum wage requirements.

6.2 DIRECT AND INDIRECT LABOUR

LEARNING SUMMARY

After studying this section you should be able to:

- calculate direct and indirect costs of labour
- describe individual and group incentive schemes.

Direct labour:

basic pay of **direct workers** (including the basic pay for any overtime)

overtime premiums when worked at a **customer's specific request**

part of the **prime cost** of a product.

Indirect labour

basic pay of **indirect workers** (for example, maintenance staff, factory supervisors and canteen staff).

indirect labour costs make up part of the **overheads** (indirect costs)

indirect labour costs also include the following:

- shift allowance or premium for night shifts or anti-social hours

- overtime premiums when due to general pressures

- bonus payments

- benefit contributions

- idle time

- sick pay

- time spent by direct workers doing 'indirect jobs'.

Overtime and overtime premiums

Overtime payments are made if employees are entitled to extra pay when hours in excess of contracted hours are worked.

KEY POINT It is important that the overtime payment is analysed correctly into direct and indirect labour costs.

Incentive schemes

Bonus schemes should be:

- **closely related to the effort** expended by employees.

- **agreed** by employers/employees before being implemented.

- **easy to understand** and simple to operate.

- **beneficial** to all of those employees taking part in the scheme

DEFINITION Premium bonus schemes pay a basic time rate, plus a portion of the time saved as compared to some agreed allowed time.

Examples of premium bonus schemes are Halsey and Rowan.

- **Halsey** – the employee receives 50% of the time saved. The bonus is calculated as:

$$\frac{\text{Time allowed} - \text{time taken}}{2} \times \text{time rate}$$

- **Rowan** - the proportion paid to the employee is based on the ratio of time taken to time allowed. The bonus is calculated as:

$$\frac{\text{Time taken}}{\text{Time allowed}} \times \text{time rate} \times \text{time saved}$$

Ensure you are able to identify the different incentive schemes and how bonuses are calculated.

- **Measured day work** – this approach pays a high time rate, but the rate is based on an analysis of past performance. Initially, work measurement is used to calculate the allowed time per unit. The allowed time is compared to the actual time taken in the past by the employee, and if this is better than the allowed time an incentive is agreed.

- **Share of production** – based on acceptance by both management and labour representatives of a constant share of value added for payroll. Any gains in value added due to improved production performance or cost savings – are shared by employees in this ratio.

6.3 LABOUR COSTS IN THE ACCOUNTING SYSTEM

LEARNING SUMMARY

After studying this section you should be able to:

- identify the methods of recording time worked
- outline the responsibilities of the payroll department
- prepare ledger entries to record labour cost inputs and outputs.

Recording time worked

Methods for recording working time

- TIME SHEETS
- JOB SHEETS
- TIME CARDS

Responsibilities of the payroll department

Responsibilities of the payroll department	Calculating **gross wages** from time and activity records.
	Calculating **net wages** after **deductions** from payroll.
	Analysis of **direct wages, indirect wages** and cash required for payment.

Accounting for labour costs

Labour costs are recorded in an organisation's statement of profit and loss. Accounting transactions relating to labour are recorded in the labour account

Labour costs paid out of the bank:

Dr Wages control account

Cr Bank

Labour costs are analysed into direct and indirect labour costs and transferred from the wages control account into appropriate accounts:

Direct labour costs are credited from the labour control account and debited in the work in progress account:

Dr Work in progress

Cr Wages control account

Indirect labour costs are credited from the labour account and debited to the production overheads account.

Dr Production overheads

Cr Wages control account

> Direct labour is directly involved in production so the cost is transferred to WIP before being transferred to finished goods and then cost of sales.

6.4 LABOUR RATIOS

LEARNING SUMMARY

After studying this section you should be able to:

* explain and calculate labour turnover, efficiency, capacity and production ratios.

Labour turnover

DEFINITION **Labour turnover** is a measure of the proportion of people leaving relative to the average number of people employed.

> Questions may require the calculation or demonstration of understanding of the meaning of ratios. Ensure you can do both.

Labour turnover is calculated as follows:

$$\frac{\text{Number of leavers who require replacement}}{\text{Average number of employees}} \times 100$$

KEY POINT Control measures might be considered if the rate of turnover seems too high.

Labour efficiency ratio

DEFINITION **Labour efficiency** measures the performance of the workforce by comparing the actual time taken to do a job with the expected or standard time.

Labour efficiency is calculated as follows:

$$\frac{\text{Standard hours for actual output}}{\text{Actual hours worked to produce output}} \times 100$$

KEY POINT Labour is a significant cost in many organisations and it is important to continually measure the efficiency of labour against pre-set targets.

Idle time ratio

DEFINITION The **idle time ratio** measures the proportion of idle time spent when productive work is not possible due to reasons such as a machinery breakdown or the resetting of a production run.

Idle time is calculated as follows:

$$\frac{\text{Idle hours}}{\text{Total hours}} \times 100$$

Labour capacity ratio

DEFINITION **Labour capacity** measures the number of hours spent actively working as a percentage of the total hours available for work (full capacity or budgeted hours).

Labour capacity is calculated as follows:

$$\frac{\text{Actual hours worked to produce output}}{\text{Total budgeted hours}} \times 100$$

Labour production volume ratio

Labour production volume is calculated as follows:

$$\frac{\text{Standard hours for actual output}}{\text{Total budgeted hours}} \times 100$$

Do you understand?

1   Outline a piecework system.

2   Under what circumstance would an overtime premium be classified as direct labour?

3   Labour capacity is a measure of the proportion of people leaving relative to the average number of people employed.

     True or false?

1   A piecework system is based on productivity, an employee is paid a fixed amount per unit produced. The total pay is calculated as: units produced x rate of pay per unit.

2   If the overtime was worked at a customer's specific request, the overtime premium would be classified as direct labour expense.

3   False, labour capacity measures the number of hours spent actively working as a percentage of the total hours available for work (full capacity or budgeted hours).

1 **How would the cost be recorded in the cost ledger if the direct labour costs in a manufacturing company are $95,000?**

    A   Debit Work-in-progress $95,000

          Credit Wages and salaries $95,000

    B   Debit Wages and salaries $95,000

          Credit Bank $95,000

    C   Debit Wages and salaries $95,000

          Credit Work-in-progress $95,000

    D   Debit Bank $95,000

          Credit Wages and salaries $95,000

2 **How would the following labour costs be classified?**

Cost	Direct	Indirect
Basic pay for production workers		
Supervisors wages		
Bonus for salesman		
Production workers overtime premium due to general pressures.		
Holiday pay for production workers		
Sick pay for supervisors		
Time spent by production workers cleaning the machinery		

3 Budgeted production in a factory for next period is 4,800 units. Each unit requires five labour hours to make. Labour is paid $10 per hour. Idle time represents 20% of the total labour time.

What is the budgeted total labour cost for the next period?

Accounting for overheads

7.1 DIRECT AND INDIRECT EXPENSES

LEARNING SUMMARY

After studying this section you should be able to:

- explain the different treatment of direct and indirect expenses.

Direct expenses

DEFINITION **Direct expenses** are expenses that can be directly identified with a specific cost unit or cost centre.

Examples of direct expenses - royalties paid to a designer or fees paid to a subcontractor for a specific job could be classed as direct expenses.

KEY POINT Direct expenses are part of the prime cost of a product.

Indirect expenses

DEFINITION **Indirect expenses** cannot be directly identified with a specific cost unit or cost centre.

Example of indirect expenses - the cost of renting a factory is classified as an indirect cost as the rent could be covering the manufacturing location of all products and also possibly other areas of the business such as the accounting department, a non-production location. It is not possible to relate the rent to a single product or location.

KEY POINT Indirect expenses are part of the overheads of a business.

7.2 PRODUCTION OVERHEADS ABSORPTION

LEARNING SUMMARY

After studying this section you should be able to:

- describe the procedures involved in determining production overhead absorption rates

- allocate and apportion production overheads to cost centres using an appropriate basis

- reapportion service cost centre costs to production cost centres

- select, apply and discuss appropriate bases for absorption rates

- prepare journal and ledger entries for manufacturing overheads incurred and absorbed

- calculate and explain the under and over absorption of overheads.

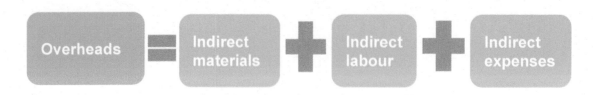

Production overheads of a factory can include; heating, lighting and renting the factory.

Production may take place over a number of different cost centres (assembly, machining and finishing) and each centre should be assigned with its fair share of overhead cost. There may also be a number of service cost centres (maintenance, canteen and stores) that provide support to the production cost centres.

Absorption costing

DEFINITION **Absorption costing** is where production overheads are recovered by absorbing them into the cost of a product.

The main aim of absorption costing is to recover overheads in a way that fairly reflects the amount of time and effort that has gone into making a product or service.

Stages of absorption costing
Allocation and apportionment of overheads to the different cost centres
Reapportionment of service (non-production) cost centre overheads to the production cost centres
Absorption of overheads into the products

Allocation and apportionment

Allocation involves charging overheads directly to specific departments (production and service).

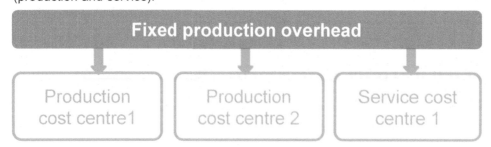

If overheads relate to more than one specific department, they must be shared between these departments using a method known as **apportionment**.

Overheads must be apportioned between different production and service departments on a fair basis.

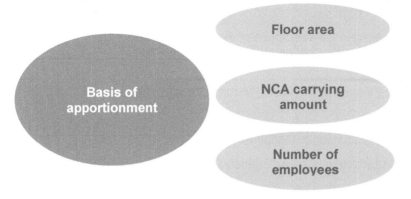

Floor area

NCA carrying amount

Number of employees

There are no hard and fast rules for which basis of apportionment to use except that whichever method is used to apportion overheads, it must be fair.

Steps of apportionment
Select an appropriate apportionment basis for each overhead cost
Calculate the overhead to be apportioned to each cost centre: $$\frac{\text{Total overhead}}{\text{Total value of apportionment basis}} \times \text{value of apportionment basis for cost centre}$$
Check that the total overhead apportioned is correct.

Reapportionment

Service cost centres (departments) are not directly involved in making products and therefore the production overheads of service cost centres must be shared out between the production cost centres (departments) using a suitable basis.

There are three methods of reapportionment

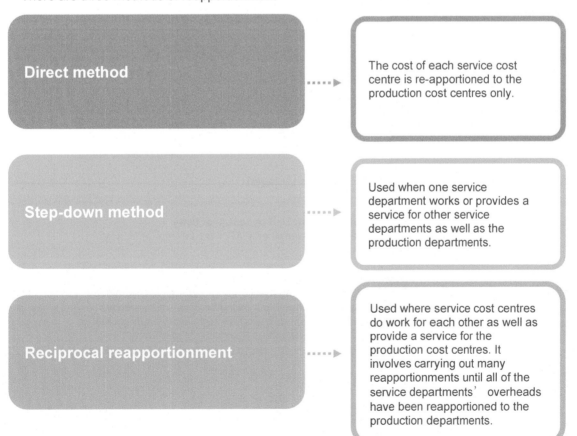

Direct method ……▷ The cost of each service cost centre is re-apportioned to the production cost centres only.

Step-down method ……▷ Used when one service department works or provides a service for other service departments as well as the production departments.

Reciprocal reapportionment ……▷ Used where service cost centres do work for each other as well as provide a service for the production cost centres. It involves carrying out many reapportionments until all of the service departments' overheads have been reapportioned to the production departments.

Absorption of overheads

The last stage in absorption costing is the absorption of the overheads into the cost units produced in the production cost centres. This is sometimes referred to as overhead recovery.

The absorption can be done on a number of bases, the most common are:

- units produced
- machine-hour rate (when production is machine intensive)
- labour-hour rate (when production is labour intensive)
- percentage of prime cost
- percentage of direct wages.

KEY POINT An overhead absorption rate is used to calculate the amount of overhead to be picked up by each unit.

Overhead absorption rate (OAR) =

$$\frac{\text{Budgeted production overhead}}{\text{Budgeted quantity of absorption base (units/labour hours/machine hours)}}$$

Under and over absorption

If the estimates for the budgeted overheads and/or the budgeted level of activity are different from the actual results for the year then this will lead to one of the following:

Under-absorption (recovery) of overheads

Over-absorption (recovery) of overheads

Calculating an under or over-absorption	
Step 1	**Calculate the OAR (based on budget)**
Step 2	**Calculate the overhead absorbed by actual activity** Overheads absorbed = predetermined OAR × actual level of activity
Step 3	**Compare absorbed to actual** If at the end of this period, the overheads absorbed are greater than the actual overheads, then there has been over-absorption of overheads. If, on the other hand, the overheads absorbed are less than the actual overheads, then there has been under-absorption of overheads.

Production overheads account

Indirect production costs are debited into the production overheads account.

Absorbed production overheads are credited out of the production overheads account and debited into the WIP account.

Any difference between the actual and absorbed overheads is known as the under- or over-absorbed overhead and is transferred to the statement of profit or loss at the end of an accounting period.

Non-production overheads are debited to one of the following:
– administration overheads account
– selling overheads account
– distribution overheads account
– finance overheads account.

Do you understand?

1   What are the three stages of absorption costing?

2   What are the three methods of reapportionment?

3   If at the end of a period the overheads absorbed are lower than the actual overheads, an over-absorption of overheads has occurred.

     True or false?

1   Allocation and apportionment, reapportionment and absorption.
2   Direct method, step-down method and reciprocal reapportionment.
3   False, if at the end of a period the overheads absorbed are lower than the actual overheads, under-absorption of overheads has occurred.

1   A factory consists of two production cost centres (G and H) and two service cost centres (J and K). The total overheads allocated and apportioned to each centre are as follows:

G	H	J	K
$40,000	$50,000	$30,000	$18,000

The work done by the service cost centres can be represented as follows:

	G	H	J	K
Percentage of service cost centre J to	30%	70%	–	–
Percentage of service cost centre K to	50%	40%	10%	–

The company apportions service cost centre costs to production cost centres using a method that fully recognises any work done by one service cost centre for another.

What are the total overheads for production cost centre G after the reapportionment of all service cost centre costs?

2   A cost centre has an overhead absorption rate of $4.25 per machine hour, based on a budgeted activity level of 12,400 machine hours.

In the period covered by the budget, actual machine hours worked were 2% more than the budgeted hours and the actual overhead expenditure incurred in the cost centre was $56,389.

What was the total over or under-absorption of overheads in the cost centre for the period?

A $1,054 over absorbed

B $2,635 under absorbed

C $3,689 over absorbed

D $3,689 under absorbed

3   **What would the accounting entries be for $10,000 of over-absorbed overheads?**

A   Dr   Work-in-progress control account

      Cr   Overhead control account

B   Dr   Statement of profit or loss

      Cr   Work-in-progress control account

C   Dr   Statement of profit or loss

      Cr   Overhead control account

D   Dr   Overhead control account

      Cr   Statement of profit or loss

8 **Absorption and marginal costing**

The following topics are covered in this chapter:
- The treatment of fixed production costs
- Marginal costing
- Absorption costing
- Impacts on inventory valuation and profit determination
- Advantages and disadvantages of absorption and marginal costing

8.1 THE TREATMENT OF FIXED PRODUCTION COSTS

LEARNING SUMMARY

After studying this section you should be able to:

- outline how fixed production costs are treated under marginal and absorption costing.

Marginal and absorption costing are two different ways of valuing the cost of goods sold and finished goods in inventory.

- **Marginal costing** treats all fixed overheads as period costs which are charged in full against the profit for the period.

- **Absorption costing** treats production overheads as a product cost and an amount is assigned to each unit.

8.2 MARGINAL COSTING

After studying this section you should be able to:

- outline what marginal costing is

- explain the importance of, and apply, the concept of contribution

The marginal cost of a unit of inventory is the total of the variable costs required to produce the unit (the marginal cost). Variable costs include:

- direct materials

- direct labour

- direct expenses

- variable production overheads

No fixed overheads are included in the inventory valuation; they are treated as a period cost and deducted in full lower down the statement of profit or loss.

DEFINITION The marginal production cost is the cost of one unit of product or service which would be avoided if that unit were not produced, or which would increase if one extra unit were produced.

KEY POINT Marginal costing is the principal costing technique used in decision making, allowing management's attention to be focused on the changes which result from the decision under consideration.

The contribution concept

The idea of calculating profit per unit is not a particularly useful one as it depends on how many units are sold. Alternatively contribution can be calculated.

KEY POINT Contribution is calculated as:

Contribution = Sales value – Variable costs

Contribution gives an idea of how much 'money' there is available to 'contribute' towards paying for the fixed costs of the organisation.

At varying levels of output and sales, profit per unit varies whereas contribution per unit is constant.

KEY POINT

Profit = Total contribution – Fixed overheads.

8.3   ABSORPTION COSTING

LEARNING SUMMARY

After studying this section you should be able to:

- outline what absorption costing is.

Absorption costing values each unit of inventory at the cost incurred to produce the unit. This includes an amount added to the cost of each unit to represent the production overheads incurred by that product. The amount added to each unit is based on estimates made at the start of the period.

KEY POINT Absorption costing is a method of building up a full product cost which adds direct costs and a proportion of production overhead costs by means of one or a number of overhead absorption rates.

8.4   IMPACTS ON INVENTORY VALUATION AND PROFIT DETERMINATION

LEARNING SUMMARY

After studying this section you should be able to:

- outline how marginal and absorption costing impacts inventory valuation and profit determination

- calculate profit or loss under absorption and marginal costing

- reconcile the profits or losses calculated under absorption and marginal costing.

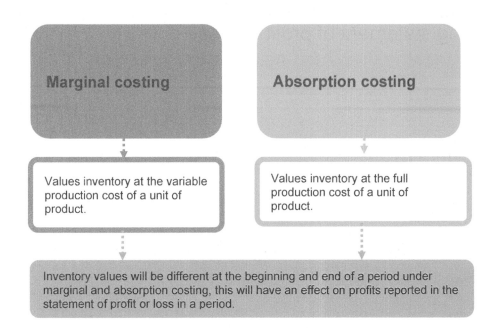

Absorption costing statement of profit or loss

	$	$
Sales		X
Less: Cost of sales:		
Opening inventory	X	
Variable cost of production	X	
Fixed overhead absorbed	X	
Less closing inventory	(X)	
		(X)
		X
(under)/over-absorption		(X)/X
Gross profit		X
Less Non-production costs		(X)
Profit/loss		X

- **Valuation of inventory** – opening and closing inventory are valued at full production cost under absorption costing.

- **Under and over-absorbed overhead** – adjustments for under or over absorption of overheads is necessary in absorption costing statements.

- **Absorption costing statements** – split into production costs in the cost of sales and non-production costs after gross profit.

Marginal costing statement of profit or loss

	$	$
Sales		X
Less: Cost of sales:		
Opening inventory	X	
Variable cost of production	X	
Less closing inventory	(X)	
		(X)
		X
Less: other variable costs		(X)
Contribution		X
Less: fixed costs		(X)
Profit/loss		X

- **Valuation of inventory** – opening and closing inventory are valued at marginal (variable) cost under marginal costing.

- **The fixed costs incurred** are deducted from contribution earned in order to determine the profit for the period.

- **Marginal costing statements** are split into all variable costs before contribution and all fixed costs after contribution.

KEY POINT Only the production variable costs are included in the cost of sales and valuation of inventory. If there are variable non-production costs (i.e. selling costs) these would be deducted before contribution but not included in the cost of sales.

Reconciling profits under the different methods

In a period where more or less inventory is produced than is sold, inventory levels will change and the profits under marginal and absorption costing will differ.

If inventory levels increase, absorption costing gives a higher profit. ·····▷ Fixed overheads held in closing inventory are carried forward (thereby reducing cost of sales) to the next accounting period instead of being written off in the current accounting period (as a period cost) as in marginal costing.

If inventory levels decrease, marginal costing gives a higher profit. ·····▷ Fixed overheads brought forward in opening inventory are released, thereby increasing cost of sales and reducing profits.

If inventory levels are constant, both methods give the same profit.

8.5 ADVANTAGES AND DISADVANTAGES OF ABSORPTION AND MARGINAL COSTING

LEARNING SUMMARY

After studying this section you should be able to:

- describe the advantages and disadvantages of absorption and marginal costing.

Marginal costing	
Advantages	**Disadvantages**
Simple	Fixed overheads may be significant.
Avoids arbitrary allocation and absorption of overheads.	
Better for short-term decision making.	Some direct costs may be fixed.
Profits only rise if sales rise (not production).	

Absorption costing	
Advantages	**Disadvantages**
Fixed production costs can be a significant part of total costs.	It requires arbitrary apportionment and allocation of overheads.
This method is required for financial reporting purposes.	The absorption basis may not actually drive the overhead cost.
Under/over-absorption can identify inefficient utilisation	It is more complex than marginal costing.
There is an argument that in the longer term, all costs are variable.	It encourages over-production.

Do you understand?

1   Absorption costing treats production overheads as a product cost and an amount is assigned to each unit.

   True or false?

2   If inventory levels were to increase which method would give a higher profit?

   True or false?

3   How is contribution calculated?

3   Contribution = Sales value − Variable costs
2   Absorption costing gives a higher profit if inventory levels increase.
1   True.

1   PQR sells one product. The cost card for that product is given below:

	$
Direct materials	4
Direct labour	5
Variable production overhead	3
Fixed production overhead	2
Variable selling cost	3

The selling price per unit is $20. Budgeted fixed overheads are based on budgeted production of 1,000 units. Opening inventory was 200 units and closing inventory was 150 units. Sales during the period were 800 units and actual fixed overheads incurred were $1,500.

What was the total contribution earned during the period?

A $2,000

B $2,500

C $4,000

D $2,500

2   In a given period, the production level of an item exactly matches the level of sales.

How would the profit differ if marginal or absorption costing was used?

A   There would not be a difference

B   It would be higher under absorption costing

C   It would be lower under absorption costing

D   It would be higher under marginal costing

3   Last month a manufacturing company's profit was $2,000, calculated using absorption costing principles. If marginal costing principles had been used, a loss of $3,000 would have occurred. The company's fixed production cost is $2 per unit. Sales last month were 10,000 units.

What was last month's production (in units)?

units

9 Job, batch and process costing

The following topics are covered in this chapter:
- Different types of production
- Process costing
- Work-in-progress (WIP) and equivalent units (EUs)
- Joint and by-products

9.1 DIFFERENT TYPES OF PRODUCTION

LEARNING SUMMARY

After studying this section you should be able to:

- describe different costing systems including job and batch costing.

Costing systems

DEFINITION **Specific order costing** is the costing system used when the work done by an organisation consists of separately identifiable jobs or batches.

DEFINITION **Continuous operation costing** is the costing method used when goods or services are produced as a direct result of a sequence of continuous operations or processes, for example process and service costing.

Job costing

DEFINITION **Job costing** is a form of specific order costing and it is used when a customer orders a specific job to be done. Each job is priced separately and each job is unique.

KEY POINT The main aim of job costing is to identify the costs associated with completing the order and to record them carefully.

A unique job number is allocated to individual jobs and the costs involved in completing the job are recording on a job cost sheet or a job card.

A certain amount of profit is added to the cost of the job to calculate the selling price.

Batch costing

DEFINITION **Batch costing** is also a form of specific order costing which is very similar to job costing.

Within a batch there are a number of identical units but each batch will be different. Each batch is a separately identifiable cost unit which is given a batch number in the same way that each job is given a job number.

Each batch number will have costs allocated to it e.g. materials requisitions will be coded to a batch number to ensure that the cost of materials used is charged to the correct batch.

Upon completion of a batch the unit cost of individual items in the batch is calculated:

$$\text{Cost per unit in batch} = \frac{\text{Total production cost of batch}}{\text{Number of units in batch}}$$

The selling price of a batch is calculated by adding profit to the cost of the batch, as seen for job costing.

KEY POINT Batch costing is very common in the engineering component industry, footwear and clothing manufacturing industries where identical items are produced; for example a batch could contain 100 pairs of size 4 shoes for a retail outlet.

9.2 PROCESS COSTING

LEARNING SUMMARY

After studying this section you should be able to:

- outline process costing.

DEFINITION Process costing is the costing method applicable when goods or services result from a sequence of continuous or repetitive operations or processes.

Process costing is used when a company is mass producing the same item and the item goes through a number of different stages. Process costing is an example of continuous operation costing.

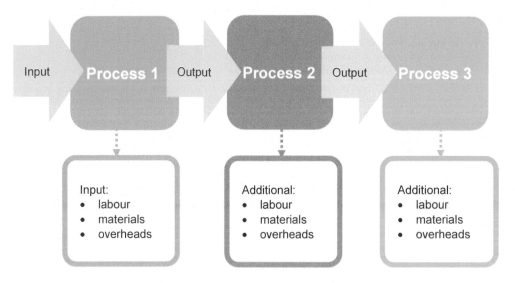

Examples include the chemical, cement, oil refinery, paint and textile industries.

One of the features of process costing is that in most process costing environments the products are identical and indistinguishable from each other. For this reason, an average cost per unit is calculated for each process.

$$\text{Average cost per unit} = \frac{\text{Net costs of inputs}}{\text{Expected output}}$$

Expected output is what we expect to get out of the process.

The output of one process forms the material input of the next process and when there is closing work-in-progress (WIP) at the end of one period, this forms the opening WIP at the beginning of the next period.

Proforma process accounts:

Process 1 account			
Materials	X	Output to process 2	X
Labour	X		
Overheads	X		
	X		X

Process 2 account			
Input materials from process 1	X	Output to process 3	X
New materials	X		
Labour	X		
Overheads	X		
	X		X

Normal losses

Losses can occur due to the evaporation or wastage of materials and this may be an expected part of the process.

Losses may sometimes be sold and generate revenue which is generally referred to as scrap proceeds or scrap value.

Normal loss and scrap value

The formula for calculating the average cost of the units output does not really change – simply the costs of inputs are reduced by the revenue received from the scrap that is sold i.e. giving the net cost.

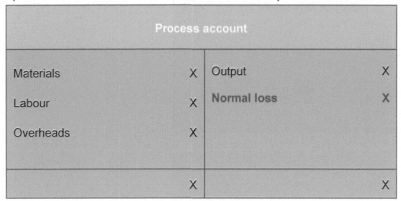

$$\text{Average cost per unit} = \frac{\text{Total costs of inputs} - \text{scrap value of normal loss}}{\text{Input units} - \text{normal loss units}}$$

Does the normal loss have a scrap value? Yes – value it at this value in the process account. No – it is valued as nil in the process account.

Process account			
Materials	X	Output	X
Labour	X	**Normal loss**	X
Overheads	X		
	X		X

Abnormal losses and gains

If the loss in a process is different to what we are expecting then we have an abnormal loss or an abnormal gain in the process.

- Abnormal loss = more loss than expected
- Abnormal gain = less loss than expected

Abnormal losses and gains and the process account

The costs associated with producing abnormal losses or gains are not absorbed into the cost of good output. Abnormal loss and gain units are valued at the same cost as units of good output in the process account.

Abnormal losses and gains and the scrap account

Losses and gains are transferred from the process account to the abnormal loss/gain account. If there is no scrap value the losses or gains are transferred to the statement of profit or loss at the value given in the process account.

If there is a scrap value then:

- the abnormal loss is transferred from the abnormal loss/gain account to the scrap account at the scrap value. The cost of the loss transferred to the statement of profit or loss is reduced by the scrap value of these loss units and the cash received for scrap sales is increased by the same amount.

- the abnormal gain is transferred from the abnormal loss/gain account to the scrap account at the scrap value. The saving associated with the gain is transferred to the statement of profit or loss but it also reduces the cash received for the scrap sale.

Process account			
Materials	X	Output	X
Labour	X	Normal loss	X
Overheads	X	**Abnormal loss**	X
	X		X

Abnormal loss account			
Process cost (AL)	X	Statement of profit or loss	X
	X		X

Recording of abnormal loss

KEY POINT This is the account where the value of the abnormal loss is recorded and the cost is transferred to the statement of profit or loss.

Process account			
Materials	X	Output	X
Labour	X	Normal loss	X
Overheads	X		
Abnormal gain	X		
	X		X

Abnormal gain account			
Statement of profit or loss	X	Process account (AG)	X
	X		X

Recording of abnormal gain

KEY POINT This is the account where the value of the abnormal gain is recorded which is also transferred to the statement of profit or loss.

Approach for answering normal loss, abnormal loss/gain questions

Calculate any normal loss units.

Draw the process account and enter the units or produce a flow of units (input units = output units). The balancing figure for the units is either an abnormal loss or gain.

Value the inputs.

Value the normal loss (if any).

Calculate the average cost per unit:

$$\frac{\text{Net costs of input}}{\text{Expected output}}$$

Value the good output and abnormal loss or gain at this average cost per unit.

Transfer the normal loss to the scrap account (if any).

Transfer the abnormal loss or gain to the abnormal loss/gain account.

Transfer the abnormal loss or gain to the scrap account at the scrap value (if any).

Balance the abnormal loss/gain account and the scrap account.

9.3 WORK-IN-PROGRESS (WIP) AND EQUIVALENT UNITS (EUs)

LEARNING SUMMARY

After studying this section you should be able to:

• understand how to account for work in progress and equivalent units.

DEFINITION **Closing work in progress (or CWIP) units** are units that have entered a production process but the process has not been completed at the end of an accounting period.

At the end of a period the output will consist of:

Fully-processed units

Partly-processed units (CWIP)

KEY POINT CWIP units become the Opening WIP (OWIP) units in the next accounting period.

It would not be fair to allocate a full unit cost to part-processed units and so we need to use the concept of equivalent units (EUs) which spreads out the process costs of a period fairly between the fully-processed and part-processed units.

Concept of equivalent units

| Equivalent unit concept | ┄┄┄┄> | Process costs are allocated to units of production on the basis of EUs - a part-processed unit can be expressed as a proportion of a fully-completed unit. | e.g. if 100 units are exactly half-way through the production process, they are effectively equal to 50 fully-completed units. |

Different degrees of completion

A process involves direct materials and conversion costs (direct labour and overheads).

Usually, all the material is put in at the beginning of the process, whereas the conversion is 'added' as the product advances through the process. This means there may be a different amount of equivalent units for conversion and materials i.e. different degrees of completion.

A step by step approach is:

Balance the units (there will be no losses in the questions you are set).

Calculate the EU for each element of cost – material, labour and overheads.

Calculate total costs for each element of cost – material, labour and overheads.

Calculate cost per EU for each element of cost.

Calculate the value of the outputs.

Opening work in progress (OWIP)

If OWIP is present there are two methods that can be used to calculate the equivalent units and calculate the cost per equivalent unit:

- **Weighted average method**
- **First in, first out (FIFO) method.**

Weighted average method

KEY POINT The weighted average method makes no distinction between units in the process at the start of a period and those added during the period. Opening inventory costs are added to current costs to provide an overall average cost per unit.

Imagine a bottle with some water in at the end of a period, when more water is added to the bottle it is not possible to tell which 'bit' of water was present as OWIP and what is 'new' water. The OWIP and material input into the process have mixed together.

KEY POINT The FIFO method assumes the OWIP units need to be completed first before any more units can be started, for example on a car production line.

Therefore:

- completed output is made up of OWIP that has been finished in the period and units that have been made from beginning to end in the period

- if OWIP units are 75% complete with respect to materials and 40% complete with respect to labour, only 25% more work will need to be carried out with respect to materials and 60% with respect to labour

- the brought forward OWIP costs are not considered to be a period cost so are not included in the EU table. They are used in the final valuation of the completed units

KEY POINT Process costs in the period must be allocated between:

– OWIP units

– units started and completed in the period (fully-worked units)

– CWIP units.

Losses made part way through production

It is possible for losses or gains to be identified part way through a process. In such a case, EUs must be used to assess the extent to which costs were incurred at the time at which the loss/gain was identified.

9.4   JOINT AND BY-PRODUCTS

LEARNING SUMMARY

After studying this section you should be able to:

- outline what joint and by-products are and how they are accounted for.

Due to the nature of process costing, the processes often produce more than one product. Additional products can be described as:

- **joint products** - main products where two or more products separated in the course of processing, each having a sufficiently high saleable value to merit recognition as a main product.

- **by-products** - incidental to the main products with outputs of some value produced incidentally in manufacturing something else (main products).

KEY POINT The distinction between joint and by-products is important because of the differences in accounting treatment.

Accounting treatment of joint and by-products

Joint products

Joint process costs occur before the split-off point. The joint costs need to be apportioned between the joint products at the split-off point to obtain the cost of each of the products in order to value closing inventory and cost of sales.

The basis of apportionment of joint costs to products is usually one of the following:

- sales value of production (also known as market value)

- production units

- net realisable value.

By-products

By-products are of less significance than the main products and may not require precise cost allocation.

Factors that can influence the valuation and accounting treatment of by-products:

- Is the value of the by-product known at the time of production?

- Could the by-product be used in other production?

- Is the by-product an alternative to the main products?

- Is there a need for separate profit calculations for sales incentives or for control?

Non-cost methods

Non-cost methods make no attempt to allocate joint cost to the by-product but instead the proceeds either increase income or to reduce the cost of the main product.

- Other income – The net sales of by-products for the current period is recognised as other income and is reported in the statement of profit or loss.

- By-product revenue deducted from the main product(s) cost – The net sales value of the by-products will be treated as a deduction from the cost of the main product(s). This is similar to the accounting treatment of normal loss.

Cost methods

Cost methods attempt to allocate some joint costs to by-products and to carry inventories at the allocated cost levels.

- Replacement cost method – values the by-product inventory at its opportunity cost of purchasing or replacing the by-products.

- Total costs less by-products valued at standard price method – By-products are valued at a standard price to avoid fluctuations in by-product value. This means that the main product cost will not be affected by any fluctuations in the by-product price.

- Joint cost pro-rata method – allocates some of the joint cost to the by-product using any one of the joint cost allocation methods. This method is rarely used in practice.

Process accounts for joint and by-products

You may be required to deal with joint and by-products when preparing process accounts. Joint products should be treated as 'normal' output from a process.

The treatment of by-products in process accounts is similar to the treatment of normal loss:

- The by-product income is credited to the process account and debited to a by-product account.

To calculate the number of units in a period, by-product units (like normal loss) reduce the number of units output. The cost per unit is calculated as:

$$\frac{\text{Process costs (materials \& conversion costs)} - \text{scrap value of normal loss} - \text{sales value of by-product}}{\text{Expected number of units output (Input units - Normal loss units - By-product units)}}$$

OR

$$\frac{\text{Net costs of input}}{\text{Expected output}}$$

Do you understand?

1. Batch costing is a form of continuous operation costing.

   True or false?

2. X uses process costing. In Process 3 the normal loss is 4% of total input.

   Last period the input from Process 2 was 8,500 kg and additional material of 4,250 kg was added to process 3.

   Actual output to finished goods was 12,700 kg.

   There was no opening or closing work-in-progress in the period.

   What was the abnormal gain or loss in kg for period 3?

   A 460 kg gain

   B 460 kg loss

   C 290 kg gain

   D 290 kg loss

3. A company operates a job costing system. Job 874 requires 110 hours of labour at $8 per hour. Materials and other expenses amount to $1,700. There are 3 employees whose basic hours are 30 hours a week. All work is to be completed in one week at the specific request of the customer. Overtime is paid at time and a quarter.

   What is the total direct labour cost of Job 874?

   A $880

   B $920

   C $2,580

   D $2.620

---

1 False. Batch costing is a form of specific order costing.

2 A

	kg	
Input	12,750	
Output	510	Normal loss
Finished goods	12,700	
	13,210	
Abnormal gain	460	

3 B

Basic hours = $110 \times \$8 =$ $880

Overtime hours = $110 - (3 \times 30) =$ 20 hours

Overtime premium = $20 \times 8 \times 0.25 =$ $40

Total direct labour cost = $\$880 + \$40 =$ $920

1   A company uses process costing to value output. During the last
    month the following information was recorded:

    Output: 2,800 kg valued at $7.50/kg

    Normal loss: 300 kg which has a scrap value of $3/kg

    Abnormal gain: 100 kg

    What was the value of the input?

$

2   A company that operates a process costing system had work-in-
    progress at the start of last month of 300 units (valued at $1,710) that
    were 60% complete in respect of all costs.

    Last month a total of 2,000 units were completed and transferred to
    the finished goods warehouse. The cost per equivalent unit for costs
    arising last month was $10. The company uses the FIFO method of
    cost allocation.

    **What was the total value of the 2,000 units transferred to the
    finished goods warehouse last month?**

    A $19,910

    B $20,000

    C $20,510

    D $21,710

3   A factory manufactures model cars. During October work commenced
    on 110,000 new cars. This was in addition to 20,000 that were 50%
    complete at the start of the month. At the end of October there were
    40,000 cars that were 50% complete.

    Costs for October were:

	$000
Brought forward	11,000
Incurred this period	121,000
	$132,000

    **If this factory chooses the weighted average method of
    spreading costs, what is the cost per car for October
    production?**

    A $1,100

    B $1,200

    C $1,210

    D $1,320

10.1 THE NATURE OF SERVICE AND OPERATION COSTING

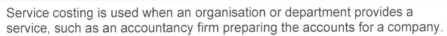

LEARNING SUMMARY

After studying this section you should be able to:

- understand the nature of service and operation costing
- outline how the service industry differs from manufacturing.

Service costing is used when an organisation or department provides a service, such as an accountancy firm preparing the accounts for a company.

The output from a service industry differs from manufacturing for the following reasons:

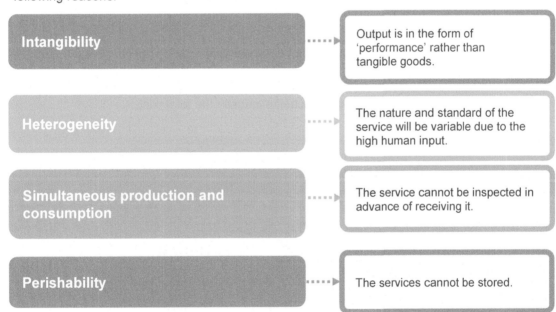

Intangibility	Output is in the form of 'performance' rather than tangible goods.
Heterogeneity	The nature and standard of the service will be variable due to the high human input.
Simultaneous production and consumption	The service cannot be inspected in advance of receiving it.
Perishability	The services cannot be stored.

10.2 SUITABLE UNIT COST MEASURES FOR SERVICE/OPERATION COSTING

LEARNING SUMMARY

After studying this section you should be able to:

- identify suitable unit cost measures for service/operation costing
- outline the total costs of providing a service
- calculate the cost per service unit.

Service organisations may use several different cost units to measure the different kinds of service that they are providing. Establishing a cost unit is one of the main difficulties in service costing.

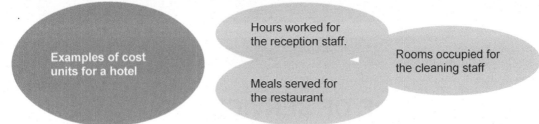

Examples of cost units for a hotel

Hours worked for the reception staff.

Meals served for the restaurant

Rooms occupied for the cleaning staff

A **composite cost unit** is more appropriate if a service is a function of two variables.

Examples of composite cost units

How much is carried over what distance (tonne-miles) for haulage companies

How many passengers travel how many miles (passenger-miles) for public transport companies..

How many patients are treated for how many days (patient-days) for hospitals.

Costs per service unit

As seen for products produced in the manufacturing industry the total cost for providing a service will include:

	$
Direct material	X
Direct labour	X
Direct expenses	X
Overheads absorbed	X
TOTAL COST	X

KEY POINT It is not uncommon for labour to be the only direct cost involved in providing a service and for overheads to make up most of the remaining total costs.

In service costing, costs can be classified as being fixed, variable or semi-variable. If costs are semi-variable, it is necessary to separate them into their fixed and variable constituents using the high/low method.

KEY POINT

Cost per service unit =

Total costs for providing the service
Number of service units used to provide the service

If organisations in the same industry use the same service units, comparisons can be made easily.

Do you understand?

1. How does the output from a service industry differ to that of a manufacturing industry?

2. What makes up the total cost of a service?

3. It is not uncommon for materials to be the only direct cost involved in providing a service. True or false?

1. Intangibility – output of a service industry is the performance rather than tangible goods.
   Heterogeneity – due to high human input in a service the nature and standard of the service varies.
   Simultaneous production and consumption – a service cannot be inspected prior to receiving it.
   Perishability – a service cannot be stored.

2. The total cost of a service includes; direct material, direct labour, direct expenses and overheads absorbed.

3. False - it is not uncommon for labour to be the only direct cost involved in providing a service and for overheads to make up most of the remaining total costs.

1 **Which of the following is NOT likely to be used in a hospital run by a charitable foundation?**

A   Cost per patient

B   Cost per bed-day

C   Bed throughput

D   Profit per patient

2 **Which TWO of the following are characteristics of service costing?**

A   High levels of indirect costs as a proportion of total cost

B   Use of equivalent units

C   Use of composite cost units

D   Long timescale from commencement to completion of the cost unit

3 **Which of the following are features of service organisations?**

(i)   High levels of inventory

(ii)   High proportion of fixed costs

(iii)   Difficulty in identifying suitable cost units

A   (i) and (ii) only

B   (i) and (iii) only

C   (ii) and (iii) only

D   All of these

11 Alternative costing principles

The following topics are covered in this chapter:

- Modern production environments
- Activity based costing
- Target costing
- Life cycle costing
- Total quality management

11.1 MODERN PRODUCTION ENVIRONMENTS

LEARNING SUMMARY

After studying this section you should be able to:

- identify the reasons why modern manufacturing differs from traditional manufacturing.

How does modern manufacturing differ from traditional manufacturing?

Smaller batch sizes are manufactured at the request of customers.

More machinery and computerised manufacturing systems are used.

Less use of 'direct' labour due to the higher use of computers and machinery.

These differences impact production costs as there are more indirect costs and less direct labour costs.

11.2 ACTIVITY BASED COSTING (ABC)

LEARNING SUMMARY

After studying this section you should be able to:

- explain activity based costing.

DEFINITION Activity based costing (ABC) is an alternative approach to product costing. It is a form of absorption costing, but, rather than absorbing overheads on a production volume basis it firstly allocates them to cost pools before absorbing them into units using cost drivers.

A **cost pool** is an activity that consumes resources and for which overhead costs are identified and allocated. For each cost pool there should be a cost driver.

A **cost driver** is a unit of activity that consumes resources. An alternative definition of a cost driver is the factor influencing the level of cost.

Advantages and disadvantages of ABC

Advantages	Disadvantages
More accurate cost per unit.	Limited benefit if the overhead costs are primarily volume related or if the overhead is a small proportion of the overall cost.
Better insight into what causes overhead costs.	Impossible to allocate all overhead costs to specific activities.
Recognises that overhead costs are not all related to production and sales volume.	Choice of both activities and cost drivers might be inappropriate.
Overhead costs can be controlled by managing cost drivers.	Can be more complex to explain to the stakeholders of the costing exercise.
Can be applied to all overhead costs, not just production overheads.	Benefits obtained might not justify the costs.
Can be used just as easily in service costing as in product costing.	

11.3 TARGET COSTING

LEARNING SUMMARY

After studying this section you should be able to:

- explain target costing.

DEFINITION **Target Costing** is a proactive cost control system. The target cost is calculated by deducting the target profit from a pre-determined selling price based on customers' views.

Step 1: A target price is set, based on the customers' perceived value of the product. This will be a market based price.

Step 2: The required target operating profit per unit is then calculated. This may be based on either return on sales or return on investment of the product.

Step 3: The target cost is derived by subtracting the target profit from the target price.

Step 4: The cost gap is then calculated.

Step 5: If there is a cost gap, attempts will be made to close the gap with techniques such as value engineering which will look at every aspect of the value chain business function.

11.4 LIFE CYCLE COSTING

After studying this section you should be able to:

- explain life cycle costing.

DEFINITION   Life cycle costing tracks and accumulates the actual costs and revenues attributable to each product from inception to abandonment. This is a technique which compares the revenues from a product with all the costs incurred over the entire product life cycle.

Sales/profit

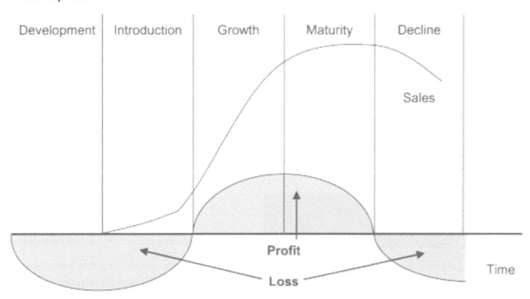

Stage	Activity
Development	The product is not yet being sold. Sales are nil and development costs are creating a loss.
Introduction	The product is launched on to the market. Sales volume is likely to be at a low level during this stage whilst the product establishes itself in the market place. Potential customers may not be fully aware of the existence of the product or may be reluctant to try a new product, preferring to remain loyal to the products already established in the market place.
Growth	It is hoped that sales volume will increase rapidly as consumers become more familiar with the product and it begins to take over from existing products in the market.
Maturity	At some point the growth in sales will slow and probably stop. The product has now reached the maturity stage in its life cycle. Sales are still at a high level. At this stage some form of modification may be required to prevent the product from going into the final stage.
Decline	Sales will fall, perhaps slowly at first, but the pace of decline is likely to increase. The product may have become outdated or unfashionable, or new products may have entered the market and attracted customers away.

11.5 TOTAL QUALITY MANAGEMENT

LEARNING SUMMARY

After studying this section you should be able to:

- explain total quality management.

DEFINITION Total quality management (TQM) is a philosophy of quality management and cost management that has a number of important features.

• **Total** – means that everyone in the value chain is involved in the process, including employees, customer and suppliers.

• **Quality** – products and services must meet the customers' requirements.

• **Management** – quality is actively managed rather than controlled so that problems are prevented from occurring.

KEY POINT One of the main aims of TQM is to achieve zero rejects and 100% quality.

There are three principles of TQM:

| Get it right, first time | Costs of prevention are less than the costs of correction. |

| Continuous improvement | The management and staff should believe that it is always possible to improve next time. |

| Customer focus | Quality is examined from a customer perspective and the system is aimed at meeting customer needs and expectations. |

Quality costs

DEFINITION A quality-related cost is the cost of ensuring and assuring quality as well as the loss incurred when quality is not achieved.

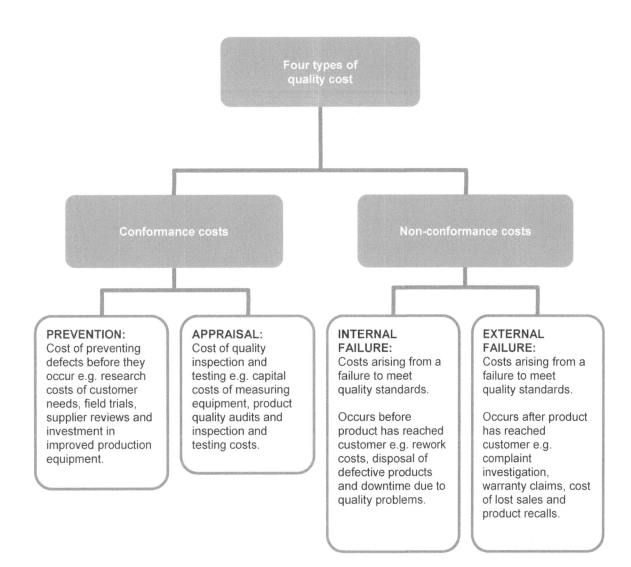

Four types of quality cost

Conformance costs

PREVENTION:
Cost of preventing defects before they occur e.g. research costs of customer needs, field trials, supplier reviews and investment in improved production equipment.

APPRAISAL:
Cost of quality inspection and testing e.g. capital costs of measuring equipment, product quality audits and inspection and testing costs.

Non-conformance costs

INTERNAL FAILURE:
Costs arising from a failure to meet quality standards.

Occurs before product has reached customer e.g. rework costs, disposal of defective products and downtime due to quality problems.

EXTERNAL FAILURE:
Costs arising from a failure to meet quality standards.

Occurs after product has reached customer e.g. complaint investigation, warranty claims, cost of lost sales and product recalls.

Do you understand?

1   What are the different stages of the lifecycle of a product?

2   State the two quality conformance costs.

3   What are the three principles of total quality management?

4   Activity based costing is a proactive cost control system. The cost is calculated by deducting the target profit from a pre-determined selling price based on customers' views.

   True or false?

1   Development, introduction, growth, maturity and decline.
2   Prevention and appraisal costs.
3   Get it right, first time, Continuous improvement and Customer focus.
4   False – target costing is a proactive cost control system. The target cost is calculated by deducting the target profit from a pre-determined selling price based on customer's views.

1   Quality control costs can be categorised into internal and external
    failure costs, inspection costs and prevention costs.

    **In which of these four classifications would the following costs
    be included?**

    • The costs of a customer service team

    • The cost of equipment maintenance

    • The cost of operating test equipment

Cost	Internal failure costs	External failure costs	Inspection costs	Prevention costs
The costs of a customer service team				
The cost of equipment maintenance				
The cost of operating test equipment				

2   The selling price of product K is set at $450 for each unit and the
    company requires a return of 20% from the product.

    What is the target cost for each unit for the coming year?

    A $300

    B $360

    C $400

    D $450

3   **What is the correct order for the stages of the product life cycle?**

    (i)   Growth

    (ii)   Decline

    (iii)   Maturity

    (iv)   Development

    (v)   Introduction

    A   (i), (v), (iii), (iv), (ii)

    B   (v), (iv), (i), (iii), (ii)

    C   (iv), (v), (i), (iii), (ii)

    D   (iv), (i), (iv), (iii), (ii)

12 Statistical techniques

The following topics are covered in this chapter:

- Forecasts in budgeting
- Regression analysis
- Correlation
- Time series analysis
- Indexes

12.1 FORECASTS IN BUDGETING

LEARNING SUMMARY

After studying this section you should be able to:

- understand the purpose of forecasting
- identify possible forecasting techniques.

The purpose of forecasting in the budgeting process is to establish realistic assumptions for planning. Forecasts may be needed for budgeting:

- the volume of output and sales
- sales revenue – volume and prices
- costs.

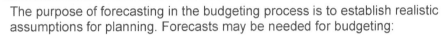

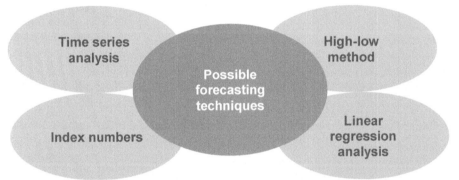

12.2 REGRESSION ANALYSIS

LEARNING SUMMARY

After studying this section you should be able to:

- understand what regression analysis is and outline the methods available to identify the relationship between two variables
- outline the benefits and limitations of linear regression.

DEFINITION Regression analysis is concerned with establishing the relationship between a number of variables.

Methods available to identify the relationship between two variables	
1	Draw a scatter diagram and plot a line of best fit
2	The high-low method (chapter 4)
3	Least squares regression analysis

Draw a scatter diagram and draw a line of best fit

The data is plotted on a graph. The y-axis represents the dependent variable, i.e. that variable that depends on the other. The x-axis shows the independent variable, i.e. that variable which is not affected by the other variable.

From the scatter diagram, the line of best fit can be estimated. The aim is to use our judgement to draw a line through the middle of data with the same slope as the data.

Least squares regression analysis

Regression analysis finds the line of best fit computationally rather than by estimating the line on a scatter diagram. It seeks to minimise the distance between each point and the regression line.

KEY POINT The equation of a straight line:

$y = a + bx$

where:

y = dependent variable

x = independent variable

a = intercept on y-axis

b = gradient of the line

and

$$b = \frac{n\sum xy - \sum x \sum y}{n\sum x^2 - (\sum x)^2}$$

where:

n = number of pairs of data

$a = \bar{y} - b\,\bar{x}$

> The equations are provided on the formulae sheet in the examination but you must have an understanding of what the letters represent and how to use the equation.

Least squares regression analysis

Linear regression analysis can be used to make forecasts or estimates whenever a linear relationship is assumed between two variables, and historical data is available for analysis.

- If the value of x is within the range of our original data, the prediction is known as Interpolation.

- If the value of x is outside the range of our original data, the prediction is known as Extrapolation.

Interpolated predictions are usually more reliable than extrapolated predictions.

> The regression equation can be used for predicting values of y from a given x value.

Uses of linear regression

Establish a trend line from a time series.	– The independent variable (x) in a time series is time.
	– The dependent variable (y) is sales, production volume or cost etc.
An alternative to using the high-low method of cost behaviour analysis.	It should be more accurate than the high-low method, because it is based on more items of historical data, not just a 'high' and a 'low' value.
	– The independent variable (x) in total cost analysis is the volume of activity.
	– The dependent variable (y) is total cost.
	– The value of a is the amount of fixed costs.
	– The value of b is the variable cost per unit of activity
To make a forecast for the budget.	When a linear relationship is identified and quantified using linear regression analysis, values for a and b are obtained, and these can be used to make a forecast for the budget. For example; sales budget or forecast can be prepared; total costs (or total overhead costs) can be estimated, for a budgeted level of activity.

Benefits vs limitations of linear regression

Benefits	Limitations
Simple and easy to use.	Assumes a linear relationship between the variables.
Looks at the basic relationship between two sets of data.	Only measures the relationship between two variables whereas in reality the dependent variable is affected by many independent variables.
Can be used to forecast and to produce budgets.	Only interpolated forecasts tend to be reliable. The equation should not be used for extrapolation.
Information required to complete the linear regression calculations should be readily available.	Regression assumes that the historical behaviour of the data continues into the foreseeable future.
Computer spreadsheet programmes often have a function that will calculate the relationship between two sets of data.	Interpolated predictions are only reliable if there is a significant correlation between the data.
Simplifies the budgeting process.	

12.3 CORRELATION

LEARNING SUMMARY

After studying this section you should be able to:

- understand types of correlation
- measure the degree of correlation and calculate

Regression analysis attempts to find the straight line relationship between two variables. Correlation is concerned with establishing how strong the straight line relationship is.

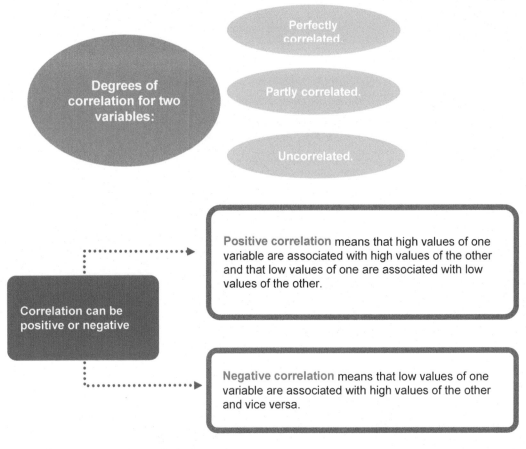

The different types of correlation are shown:

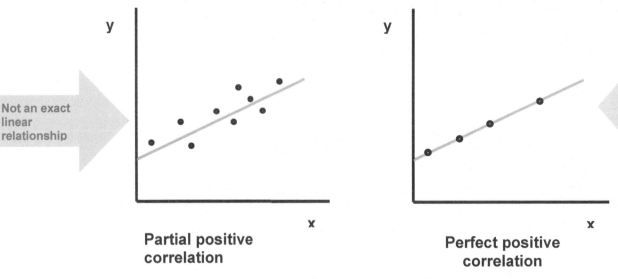

KEY POINT Although the partial positive correlation does not have an exact linear relationship high values of x tend to be associated with high values of y.

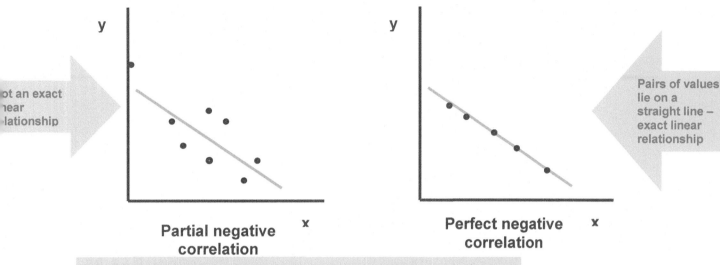

Partial negative correlation

Perfect negative correlation

KEY POINT Although the partial negative correlation does not have an exact linear relationship low values of x tend to be associated with high values of y and vice versa.

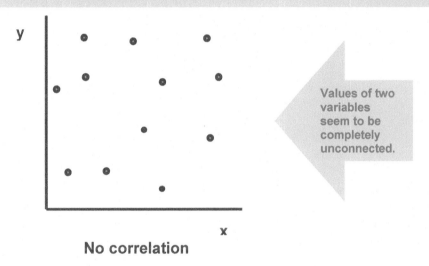

No correlation

Correlation coefficient

The degree of correlation can be measured by the Pearsonian correlation coefficient, r (also known as the product moment correlation coefficient).

$$ r = \frac{n\Sigma xy - \Sigma x \Sigma y}{\sqrt{(n\Sigma x^2 - (\Sigma x)^2)(n\Sigma y^2 - (\Sigma y)^2)}} $$

The equation is provided on the formulae sheet in the examination but you must have an understanding of what the letters represent and how to use the equation.

r always lies in the range −1 to +1, where:

r = +1 denotes perfect positive linear correlation

r = −1 denotes perfect negative linear correlation

r = 0 denotes no linear correlation

The coefficient of determination

This squares the correlation in order to express the strength of the relationship between the variables as a percentage.

The coefficient of determination, r2, gives the proportion of changes in y that can be explained by changes in x, assuming a linear relationship between x and y.

12.4 TIME SERIES ANALYSIS

DEFINITION **Time series analysis** uses moving averages to create a trend line over time, established from historical data, that, when adjusted for seasonal variations, can then be used to make predictions for the future.

Components of a time series

Trend - The long term general movement of the data.	**Seasonal variations** - A regular variation around the trend over a fixed time period, usually one year.
Cyclical variations - The economic cycle of booms and slumps.	**Residual or random variations** - Irregular, random fluctuations in the data usually caused by factors specific to the time series.

Trend

In time series analysis the trend is measured by:

Inspection	A graph of the data is produced and the trend line is drawn by eye with the aim of plotting the line so that it lies in the middle of the data points.
Least squares regression analysis	x represents time (each month would be given a number e.g. January =1, February =2 etc.) and y is the data.
Moving averages	This method attempts to remove seasonal or cyclical variations by a process of averaging.

Seasonal variations

Seasonal variations are used to forecast future figures by amending the trend. There are two main models:

The additive model - the seasonal variation is expressed as an absolute amount to be added on to the trend to find the actual result, e.g. ice-cream sales in summer are expected to be $200,000 above the trend.

Forecast = Trend + Seasonal variation

The multiplicative model - the seasonal variation is expressed as a ratio / proportion / percentage to be multiplied by the trend to arrive at the actual figure, e.g. ice-cream sales are expected to be 50% more than the trend.

Forecast = Trend x Seasonal variation

Cyclical variations

Cyclical variations are medium-term to long term influences usually associated with the economy. These cycles are rarely of consistent length and we would need 6 or 7 full cycles of data to be sure that the cycle was there.

Residual or random variations

Residual or random variations are caused by irregular items, which cannot be predicted.

DEFINITION **A moving average** is a series of averages calculated from historical time series data. By using moving averages, the variations in a time series can be eliminated leaving a 'smoothed' set of figures which is taken as the trend.

Calculating moving averages

Step 1

Choose the correct cycle length. For instance, if there are seasonal variations present in a time series and the pattern is repeated every third period (quarterly), the moving average should be calculated based on three periods at a time to get the best results. It is possible to calculate a moving average based on any length of cycle.

Step 2

Calculate the total for the first cycle.

Step 3

Calculate the average by dividing the total by the number of periods in the cycle.

Step 4

Repeat the process for the next cycle, moving on just one period.

Repeat the calculation for each successive cycle until the data has been fully analysed.

Advantages and disadvantages of time series analysis

Advantages	Disadvantages
Forecasts are based on clearly-understood assumptions.	There is an assumption that what has happened in the past is a reliable guide to the future.
Trend lines can be reviewed after each successive time period, when the most recent historical data is added to the analysis; consequently, the reliability of the forecasts can be assessed.	There is an assumption that a straight-line trend exists.
Forecasting accuracy can possibly be improved with experience.	There is an assumption that seasonal variations are constant, either in actual values using the additive model (such as dollars of sales) or as a proportion of the trend line value using the multiplicative model.

Product life cycle and forecasting

The product life cycle can also be used during the forecasting procedure. If an organisation knows where a product is in its life cycle, they can use this knowledge to plan the marketing of that product more effectively and, more importantly, the organisation may be able to derive an approximate forecast of its sales from knowledge of the current position of the product in its life cycle.

KEY POINT It is too simplistic to assume that sales will continue on a linear upward trend forever, every product eventually reaches maturity and may go on to decline.

12.5 INDEXES

LEARNING SUMMARY

After studying this section you should be able to:

- outline what an index number is

- how to calculate and use an index number

- outline the advantages and disadvantages of index numbers.

DEFINITION An **index number** is a technique for comparing, over time, changes in some feature of a group of items (e.g. price or quantity) by expressing the property each period as a percentage of some earlier period.

The year that is used as the initial year for comparison is known as the base year. The **base year** for an index should be chosen with some care. As far as possible it should be a 'typical year' therefore being as free as possible from abnormal occurrences. The base year should also be fairly recent and revised on a regular basis.

Calculating and using an index number

KEY POINT An index number is calculated as:

Current value ÷ base value × 100

Index numbers can also be used to forecast future data to be in cash flows.

KEY POINT The formula for using an index is:

Current index ÷ base index × base value

Types of indices

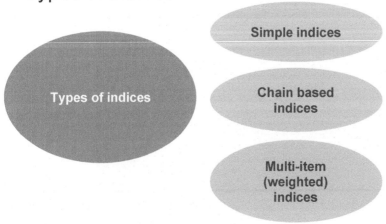

Simple indices

DEFINITION A **simple index** is one that measures the changes in either price or quantity of a single item.

Two types of simple indices:

Price index	Quantity index
Price index = $P_1 \div P_0 \times 100$	Quantity index = $Q_1 \div Q_0 \times 100$

P1 and Q1 price/quantity at time 1

P0 and Q0 – price/quantity at time 0 (base year)

Chain based indices

DEFINITION A **chain based index number** expresses each year's value as a percentage of the value for the previous year.

If a series of index numbers are required for different years, showing the rate of change of the variable from one year to the next, the chain base method is used.

This means each index number is calculated using the previous year as base. If the rate of change increases, then the index numbers will be rising; if it is constant, the numbers will remain the same and if it decreases the numbers will be falling.

Chain base index = $\dfrac{\text{This year's value}}{\text{Last year's value}} \times 100$

Multi-item (weighted) indices

DEFINITION A **weighted index** measures the change in overall price or overall quantity of a number of different items compared to the base year.

Advantages and disadvantages of index numbers

Advantages	Disadvantages
They aid the management understanding of information presented to them.	There may be no single correct way of calculating an index, especially the more sophisticated index numbers. The user of the information should bear in mind the basis on which the index is calculated.
Indices present changes in data or information over time in percentage terms.	The overall result obtained from multi-item index numbers are averages.
They make comparison between items of data easier and more meaningful – it is relatively easy to make comparisons and draw conclusions from figures when you are starting from a base of 100.	They should only be applied to the items which are included in the index calculation.
The ability to calculate separate price and quantity indices allows management to identify the relative importance of changes in each of two variables.	They are relative values, not absolute figures and may not give the whole picture.

KEY POINT The accuracy of forecasting is affected by the need to adjust historical data and future forecasts to allow for price or cost inflation.

Do you understand?

1. Using the data provided calculate the price index for 2003.

Year	Selling price ($)	Index
2000	22	100
2001	23	
2002	26	
2003	25	
2004	28	

    (i)   105

    (ii) 118

    (iii) 114

    (iv) 127

2. Regression analysis has been used to calculate the line of best fit from a series of data. Using this line to predict a value which lies between the two extreme values observed historically is known as extrapolation.

    True or false?

3. Positive correlation means that high values of one variable are associated with high values of the other and that low values of one are associated with low values of the other.

    True or false?

1   Regression analysis is being used to find the line of best fit (y = a + bx) from eleven pairs of data. The calculations have produced the following information:

Σx = 440, Σy = 330, Σx^2 = 17,986, Σy^2 = 10,366 and Σxy = 13,467

What is the value of 'b' in the equation for the line of best fit (to 2 decimal places)?

```
┌─────────────┐
│             │
│             │
└─────────────┘
```

2   The coefficient of determination (r^2) has been calculated as 60%.

What does this mean?

A   60% of the variation in the dependent variable (y) is explained by the variation in the independent variable (x)

B   40% of the variation in the dependent variable (y) is explained by the variation in the independent variable (x)

C   60% of the variation in the dependent variable (x) is explained by the variation in the independent variable (y)

D   40% of the variation in the dependent variable (x) is explained by the variation in the independent variable (y)

3   An inflation index and index numbers of a company's sales ($) for the last year are given below.

Quarter:	1	2	3	4
Sales ($) index:	109	120	132	145
Inflation index:	100	110	121	133

How are the 'Real' sales performing, i.e. adjusted for inflation?

A   approximately constant and keeping up with inflation

B   growing steadily and not keeping up with inflation

C   growing steadily and keeping ahead of inflation

D   falling steadily and not keeping up with inflation

13 Budgeting

The following topics are covered in this chapter:

- Budget preparation
- Behavioural aspects of budgeting
- Functional budgets
- Budgetary control

13.1 BUDGET PREPARATION

LEARNING SUMMARY

After studying this section you should be able to:

- explain why organisations use budgeting
- describe the planning and control cycle in an organisation
- outline the stages in budget preparation.

DEFINITION A budget is a quantitative expression of a plan of action prepared in advance of the period to which it relates.

Budgets set out the costs and revenues that are expected to be incurred or earned in future periods.

Types of budgets that can be prepared by organisations:

- **Departmental budgets.**
- **Functional budgets** (for sales, production, expenditure and so on).
- **Statements of profit or loss and Statements of financial position** (in order to determine the expected future profits).
- **Cash budgets** (in order to determine future cash flows).

Purposes of budgeting

Planning for the future	Ensure plans are in line with the objectives of the organisation.
Controlling costs	Compare the plan or the budget with the actual results and investigate significant differences between the two.
Co-ordination of the different activities	Ensures managers are working towards a common goal.
Communication	Communicate targets of the organisation to individual managers.
Motivation	Motivate to beat targets however if budgets are badly set it can demotivate employees.
Evaluation	The performance of managers is often judged by looking at how well the manager has performed 'against budget'.
Authorisation	Budgets act as a form of authorisation of expenditure.

The stages in budget preparation

A budget committee is formed.	A typical budget committee is made up of the chief executive, budget (management accountant) and departmental or functional heads (sales manager, purchasing manager, production manager and so on).
	The budget committee is responsible for communicating policy guidelines to the people who prepare the budgets and for setting and approving budgets.
A budget manual is produced.	The manual sets out instructions relating to the preparation and use of budgets.
	It gives details of the responsibilities of those involved in the budgeting process, including an organisation chart and a list of budget holders.
The limiting factor is identified.	The limiting factor is known as the principal budget factor. Usually there is one factor that will limit the activity of an organisation in a given period. It is usually sales that limit an organisation's performance, but it could be anything else, for example, the availability of special labour skills.
Final steps in the budget process:	Once the budget relating to the limiting factor has been produced then the managers responsible for the other budgets can produce them. The entire budget preparation process may take several weeks or months to complete. The final stages are as follows:
	Initial budgets are prepared. Budget managers may sometimes try to build in an element of budget slack – this is a deliberate overestimation of costs or under-estimation of revenues which can make it easier for managers to achieve their targets.
	Initial budgets are reviewed and integrated into the complete budget system.
	After any **necessary adjustments** are made to initial budgets, they are accepted and the **master budget is prepared** (budgeted statement of profit or loss, statement of financial position and cash flow). This master budget is then shown to higher management for final approval.
	Budgets are reviewed regularly. Comparisons between budgets and actual results are carried out and any differences arising are known as variances.

The preparation of budgets is illustrated as follows:

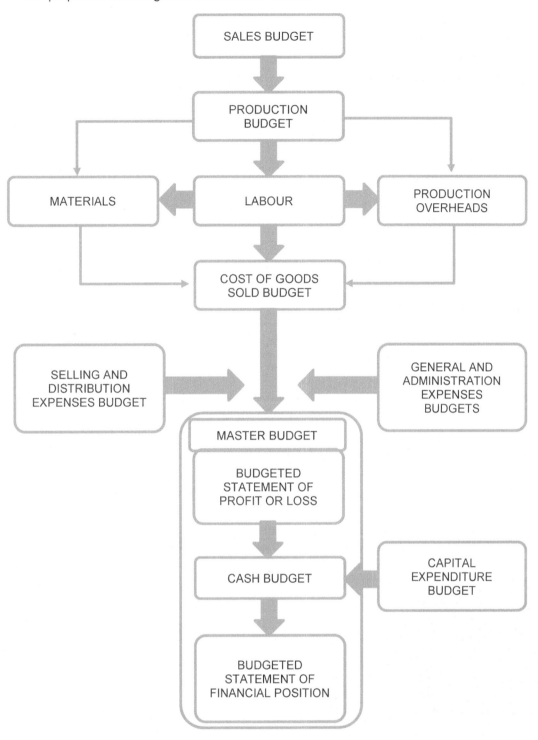

13.2 BEHAVIOURAL ASPECTS OF BUDGETING

> **DEFINITION** **Motivation** is the drive or urge to achieve an end result.

An individual is motivated if they are moving forward to achieving goals or objectives. If employees and managers are not motivated, they will lack the drive or urge to improve their performance and to help the organisation to achieve its goals and move forward.

> **KEY POINT** Motivation is very important in a business. management accounting planning and control systems can have a significant effect on manager and employee motivation.

- **If a budget target is set that is too easy**, then actual performance will appear to be better than the budget but it will not have challenged the employees.

- **If the budget is too difficult**, managers become discouraged at what they regard as an unattainable standard.

Incentive schemes

Budgets by themselves have a limited motivational effect. It is the reward structure that is linked to achieving the budget requirements, or lack of reward for non-achievement, which provides the real underlying motivational potential of budgets.

Characteristics of a good employee reward system	Understandable	Motivational
	Consistently applied	Fair
Universal	Objective	

Incentive schemes tie pay directly to performance and the reward should encourage improvements in performance. It can be tied to the performance of an individual or a team of employees. The scheme should link performance to organisational goals.

- **Long-term incentive schemes** are designed to continually motivate and deliver organisational objectives.

- **Short-term incentive schemes** motivate in the short term but do not deliver on-going motivation and are often achieved at the detriment of longer term objectives.

Types of incentive schemes

Performance related pay (PRP) ·······▸

- **Piecework** - reward related to the pace of work or effort. The faster the employee works, the higher the output and the greater the reward.
- **Management by objectives (MBO)** - key results are identified -rewards will be paid on top of the salary.
- **Points system** - this is an extension to MBO reward systems where a range of rewards is available based on a point system derived from the scale of improvement made such as the amount of cost reduction achieved.

Bonus schemes ·······▸ Usually a one off as opposed to PRP schemes which are usually a continual management policy.

Profit sharing ·······▸ Usually available to a wide group of employees (often company-wide) where payments are made in the light of the overall profitability of the company.
Share issues may be part of the scheme.

Participative budgeting

Top down approach to budgeting

DEFINITION The **top down approach** is where budgets are set by higher levels of management and then communicated to the lower levels of management to whose areas of responsibility they relate. This is also known as an imposed budget.

Lower level managers are not allowed to participate in the budget setting process. The lack of ownership of the budget may mean there is reluctance to take responsibility for it.

However, it could be argued that this top down approach may be the only approach to budgeting which is feasible if:

- lower level employees have no interest in participating in the process

- they are not technically capable of participating in budget setting

- only top level management have access to information which is necessary for budgeting purposes – perhaps information which is commercially sensitive.

Bottom up approach to budgeting

DEFINITION The **bottom up approach** to budgeting is where lower level managers are involved in setting budget targets. This is known as a participative budget.

If individual managers are involved in setting budget targets, it is likely that they will accept those targets and strive actively towards the attainment of them. Employees are more likely to internalise the budget – accept it as part of themselves.

KEY POINT If budgets are used both in a motivational role and for the evaluation of managerial performance a problem of budgetary bias may arise.

DEFINITION Budgetary bias is where a manager deliberately sets a lower revenue target or a higher cost target.

DEFINITION A continuous budget is prepared a year (or budget period) ahead and is updated regularly by adding a further accounting period (month, quarter) when the first accounting period has expired. If the budget period is a year, then it will always reflect the budget for a year in advance. Continuous budgets are also known as rolling budgets.

13.3 FUNCTIONAL BUDGETING

LEARNING SUMMARY

After studying this section you should be able to:

- prepare sales, functional, cash and master budgets
- outline 'what if' analysis and scenario planning.

DEFINITION A functional budget is a budget of income and/or expenditure which applies to a particular function of the business.

Sales budgets

For most organisations, the principal budget factor is usually sales volume. The sales budget is therefore the primary budget from which the majority of other budgets are derived.

> **The sales budget = sales volume × selling price**

Production budgets

> **Budgeted production = forecast sales + closing inventory – opening inventory**

Material budgets

The material usage budget is simply the budgeted production for each product multiplied by the quantity (e.g. kg) required to produce one unit of the product.

Materials purchases budget

> **Materials purchases budget = forecast materials usage + closing inventory – opening inventory**

Labour budgets

Labour budgets are simply the number of hours multiplied by the labour rate per hour

Overhead budgets

Overhead budgets will be based on budgeted activity and budgeted OAR

Cash budgets and cash flow forecasts

DEFINITION A cash forecast is an estimate of cash receipts and payments for a future period under existing conditions.

Cash forecasts can be prepared based on:

- **Receipts and payments forecast**. This is a forecast of cash receipts and payments based on predictions of sales and cost of sales and the timings of the cash flows relating to these items.

- **Statement of financial position forecast**. This is a forecast derived from predictions of future statements of financial position. Predictions are made of all items except cash, which is then derived as a balancing figure.

DEFINITION A cash budget is a commitment to a plan for cash receipts and payments for a future period after taking any action necessary to bring the forecast into line with the overall business plan.

Cash budgets are used to:

- assess and integrate operating budgets

- plan for cash shortages and surpluses

- compare with actual spending.

> In the exam it is most likely to be part of a receipts and payments forecast i.e. calculating the receipts from receivables or the payments to payables.

Preparing a cash budget

There is no definitive format which should be used for a cash budget. However, it should include:

A clear distinction between the cash receipts and cash payments for each period and a subtotal clearly shown for each.

A figure for the net cash flow for each period.

The closing cash balance for each period.

Note:

- **Only include cash flows** – items such as depreciation are not cash flows.

- **Allowance must be made for bad and doubtful debts** – bad debts will never be received, and doubtful debts may not be received. When you are forecasting the cash receipts from customers you must remember to adjust for these items.

- **Include all cash flows** – the cash budget does not just reflect sales revenue and production costs, but all movements of cash including cash flows for financial items such as inflows from the sale of shares or grants received and outflows such as the purchase of a non-current asset or the repayment of a loan.

Cash receipts and payments

To calculate the cash receipts from the credit sales consider:

- the value of the receipts – how much cash will be received from the credit sales?
- the timing of the receipts – when will the cash be received from the credit sales?

To calculate the cash payments from the credit purchases consider:

- the value of the payment – how much cash will be paid to the pavable?
- the timing of the payment – when will the cash be paid to the pavable?

Preparing master budgets

Having prepared budgets for sales and costs, the master budget can be summarised as a statement of profit or loss, a cash budget (and a statement of financial position as at the end of the budget period.

'What if' analysis

DEFINITION **'What-if' analysis** is a form of sensitivity analysis, which allows the effects of changes in one or more data value to be quickly recalculated.

Most budgets are quite complex, involving a large number of inputs. What-if analysis is a technique whereby each of the inputs can be changed both individually and in combination to see the effects on the final results.

Scenario planning

DEFINITION **Scenario planning** or scenario thinking is a strategic planning tool used to make flexible long-term plans. It is a strategic planning method that some organisations use to make flexible long-term plans.

The steps for scenario planning:

- Define the business question
- Identify the critical factors
- Identify the inputs
- Generate scenarios
- Develop the scenarios
- Transfer the scenarios to the business model
- Develop strategic alternatives and the strategic plan

13.4 BUDGETARY CONTROL

LEARNING SUMMARY

After studying this section you should be able to:

- define budgetary control and responsibility accounting

- understand what fixed and flexed budgets are and how they are calculated

- explain the concept of controllable and uncontrollable costs.

Budgetary control and responsibility accounting

DEFINITION Budgetary control is about assessing actual performance against budgeted performance and taking corrective action when necessary.

Budgetary control and responsibility accounting are seen to be inseparable. An area of responsibility may be structured as:

Responsibility centre:	Responsibilities of management:
Cost centre	Costs only
Revenue centre	Revenues only
Profit centre	Costs and revenues
Investment centre	Costs, revenues, investments and disposal of assets

KEY POINT In many cases it may not be obvious which centre or manager is responsible for given activities, even if a clearly defined organisation chart is in place and appropriate responsibility accounting units have been set up.

The problem of dual responsibility

The responsibility for a particular cost or item is shared between two (or more) managers. The reporting system should be designed so that the responsibility for performance achievements (i.e. better or worse than budget) is identified as that of a single manager.

If a manager controls quantity and price – that manager is responsible for all expenditure variances.

If manager controls quantity but not price – that manager is responsible only for variances due to usage.

If manager controls price but not quantity – that manager is responsible only for variances due to input prices.

If manager controls neither quantity nor price – all variances are uncontrollable from the point of view of that manager. We should now be asking the question who in the organisation chart is responsible for control of the expenditure?

Controllable and uncontrollable costs

DEFINITION **Controllable costs and revenues** are those costs and revenues which result from decisions within the authority of a particular manager or unit within the organisation. These should be used to assess the performance of managers.

Controllable costs are generally considered to be those which are variable or directly attributable fixed costs.

DEFINITION **Uncontrollable** costs are costs that cannot be influenced (i.e. their value can neither be increased nor decreased) by management action.

Fixed and flexible budgets

DEFINITION **A fixed budget** contains information on costs and revenues for one level of activity.

Where the actual level of activity is different to that expected, comparisons of actual results against a fixed budget can give misleading results.

DEFINITION **A flexible budget** is one which, by recognising cost behaviour patterns, is designed to change as volume of activity changes.

A flexible budget should represent what the costs and revenues were expected to be at different activity levels.

A flexed budget provides two key benefits:

- managers are better prepared for a range of scenarios

- variances can be based on the most suitable budget.

KEY POINT **Managers should always compare performance against a flexed budget.**

The flexed budget (budget cost allowance) is calculated as follows:

Fixed costs: no change

Variable costs:

$$\text{Budgeted cost allowance} = \frac{\text{Budgeted cost}}{\text{Budgeted activity level}} \times \text{Actual activity level}$$

Semi-variable costs: The fixed element will not change and the variable element will be flexed as above.

Do you understand?

1. Explain what is meant by a flexed budget.

2. What is the formula to calculate the production budget?

3. What is the formula to calculate the material usage budget?

4. A company makes 2 products, X and Y, which are sold in the ratio 1:2. The selling prices are $50 and $100 respectively. The company wants to earn $100,000 over the next period. What should the sales budget be?

	X (units)	Y (units)
A	1,334	667
B	800	400
C	667	1,334
D	400	800

1. An original budget is set at the beginning of the period based on the estimated level of activity. This is, then, flexed to correspond with the actual level of activity.

2. The production budget is the sales budget minus opening inventory of finished goods plus closing inventory of finished goods.

3. The material usage budget is the material requirement for the units produced.

4. D
   If 1X and 2Y are sold, this earns $250. Call this a batch.
   The company wants to earn $100,000.
   $100,000/250 = 400 batches.
   This is 400 X and 800 Y

Exam style questions

1   Oswald Press produces and sells textbooks for schools and colleges. The following budgeted information is available for the year ending 31 December 20X6:

	Budget	Actual
Sales (units)	120,000	100,000
	$000	$000
Sales revenue	1,200	995
Variable printing costs	360	280
Variable production overheads	60	56
Fixed production cost	300	290
Fixed administration cost	360	364
Profit	120	5

What does the flexed budget show?

A   a profit of $10,000

B   a loss of $10,000

C   a profit of $100,000

D   a loss of $100,000

2   The following budgeted information comes from the accounting records of Smith

	Original budget
Sales units	1,000
	$
Sales revenue	100,000
Direct material	40,000
Direct labour	20,000
Variable overhead	15,000
Fixed overhead	10,000
	————
Profit	15,000
	————

In a period where the actual sales were 1,200 units, what would be the budgeted flexed profit?

A $17,000

B $20,000

C $22,000

D $35,000

3   Mr Grob started trading in 20X3, selling one product, wheelbarrows, on credit to small retail outlets. The following budgeted information for 20X4 has been gathered:

	January 20X4	February 20X4	March 20X4
Credit sales	$12,000	$15,000	$21,000

Receivables have recently been settling their debts 50% in the month following sale, and 50% two months after sale. A prompt payment discount of 3% is offered to those receivables paying within one month.

The gross profit margin is expected to be 25%. Due to an anticipated continued increase in sales, Mr Grob intends to increase inventory levels in March 20X4 by $2,000, and it is intended that the payables balance is increased by $3,000 to ease cash flow in the same month.

Required:

(a)   Calculate the budgeted cash that will received in March 20X4.

(b)   Calculate the budgeted payment to suppliers in March 20X4

(c)   Calculate the chain base index for sales in February 20X4 and March 20X4

(d)   The following incomplete statement has been made.

The product life cycle has (gap 1) stages. Mr Grob's business is in the (gap 2) phase of the product lifecycle.

Required:

Select the correct words to complete the sentence.

Gap 1

A   Four

B   Five

Gap 2

A   Introduction

B   Growth

14 Capital budgeting

The following topics are covered in this chapter:

- Capital and revenue expenditure
- Capital budgeting and investment appraisal
- The time value of money and interest
- Capital investment appraisal

14.1 CAPITAL AND REVENUE EXPENDITURE

LEARNING SUMMARY

After studying this section you should be able to:

- define and distinguish between capital and revenue expenditure

When a business spends money on new non-current assets it is known as capital investment or capital expenditure.

Many different investment projects exist including:

- replacement of assets.

- cost-reduction schemes

- new product/service developments

- product/service expansions

- statutory, environmental and welfare proposals.

DEFINITION Capital expenditure is expenditure incurred in: the acquisition of non-current assets required for use in the business and not for resale and the alteration or significant improvement of non-current assets for the purpose of increasing their revenue-earning capacity.

Capital expenditure is initially shown in the statement of financial position as non-current assets. It is then charged to the statement of profit or loss over a number of periods, via the depreciation charge.

DEFINITION Revenue expenditure is expenditure incurred in: the purchase of assets acquired for conversion into cash (e.g. goods for resale); the manufacturing, selling and distribution of goods and the day-to-day administration of the business or the maintenance of the revenue-earning capacity of the non-current assets (i.e. repairs, etc).

Revenue expenditure is generally charged to the statement of profit or loss for the period in which the expenditure was incurred.

14.2 CAPITAL BUDGETING AND INVESTMENT APPRAISAL

LEARNING SUMMARY

After studying this section you should be able to:

- recall the stages of the capital budgeting process
- identify the cash flows relevant to investment appraisal.

The capital budgeting process consists of a number of stages:

> Forecast capital requirements.

> Identify suitable projects.

> Appraise potential projects.

> Select and approve the best alternative.

> Make capital expenditure.

> Compare actual and planned spending, investigate deviations and monitor benefits from project over time.

Cash flows used for investment appraisal

In capital investment appraisal it is more appropriate to evaluate future cash flows rather than accounting profits.

Cash flows that are appraised should be relevant to or change as a direct result of making a decision to invest. Relevant cash flows are:

- **future costs and revenues** – it is not possible to change what has happened so any relevant costs or revenues are future ones

- **cash flows** – actual cash coming in or leaving the business not including any non-cash items such as depreciation and notional costs

- **incremental costs and revenues** – the change in costs or revenues that occur as a direct result of a decision to invest.

14.3 THE TIME VALUE OF MONEY AND INTEREST

After studying this section you should be able to:

- understand how time impacts the value of money

- explain the difference between simple and compound interest, and between nominal and effective interest rates

- explain compounding and discounting.

As the cash flows relating to a capital expenditure project arise over the long term (over 12 months) it is necessary to take into consideration the time value of money.

What factors need to be taken into consideration?	
1	**Cost of finance** – if the funds were available now the cash could be used to repay or reduce a loan, in turn reducing interest charges on the loan.
2	**Investment opportunities** – the funds could be invested to earn a return, often expressed at a percentage return.
3	**Inflation** – erodes the purchasing power of the funds as prices of commodities increase.
4	**Risk** – funds received sooner are more certain.

KEY POINT All four of the factors above combine to express the time value of money as an interest rate.

Simple interest

Simple interest is calculated based on the original sum invested. Any interest earned in earlier periods is not included. Simple interest is often used for a single investment period that is less than a year.

KEY POINT The formula to calculate the future value of an amount invested under these terms is:

$V = X + (X \times r \times n)$

V – future value

X – initial investment (present value)

r – interest rate (expressed as a decimal)

n – number of time periods

Compound interest

A sum invested today will earn interest. Compounding calculates the future value of a given sum invested today for a number of years. To compound a sum, the figure is increased by the amount of interest it would earn over the period. Interest is earned on interest gained in earlier periods.

KEY POINT The formula for compounding is:

$V = X(1+r)^n$

V = Future value

X = Initial investment (present value)

r = Interest rate

n = number of time periods

Nominal interest rate

The nominal interest rate is the stated interest rate for a time period – for example a month or a year.

Effective interest rate

The effective interest rate is the interest rate that includes the effects of compounding a nominal interest rate.

> **KEY POINT** The formula to calculate the effective interest rate is as follows:
>
> $r = (1 + i/n)^n - 1$
>
> r – effective interest rate
>
> i – nominal interest rate
>
> n – number of time periods

Do you understand?

1 If $100 is invested in an account for a period of six months with an interest rate of 10% per annum, what is the value of the account after six months?

2 If $100 is invested in an account for a period of five years with an interest rate of 10% per annum, what is the value of the account after five years?

3 The nominal interest rate is 10% per annum compounded on a monthly basis. If a company is going to invest for a period of 12 months what is the effective interest rate?

1 $V = X + (X \times r \times n)$
$V = 100 + (100 \times 0.1 \times (6/12)) = \$105$
2 $V = X(1+r)^n$
$V = 100 (1.10)^5 = \$161.05$
3 $r = (1 + i/n)^n - 1$
$r = (1 + 0.1/12)^{12} - 1$
$r = 0.1047$
The effective interest rate of receiving 10% interest per annum compounded on a monthly basis for 12 months is the same as receiving 10.47% interest per annum with no compounding.

Discounting

Discounting performs the opposite function to compounding. Compounding finds the future value of a sum invested now, whereas discounting considers a sum receivable in the future and establishes its equivalent value today. This value in today's terms is known as the Present Value.

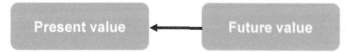

Present value (X) = $\dfrac{\text{Future value (V)}}{(1 + r)^n}$

This can be shown as:

Present value (X) = Future value (V) x $\dfrac{1}{(1 + r)^n}$

Or

Present value (X) = Future value (V) × $(1 + r)^{-n}$

Where $1 \div (1 + r)n$ or $(1 + r)-n$ is known as the discount factor

14.4 CAPITAL INVESTMENT APPRAISAL

LEARNING SUMMARY

After studying this section you should be able to:

- evaluate investments using payback, NPV and IRR
- outline the advantages and disadvantages of each appraisal method
- calculate present value using annuity and perpetuity formulae.

The payback period

Three appraisal methods:

Net present value (NPV)

Internal rate of return (IRR)

Ensure you are comfortable with the calculations for each appraisal method.

KEY POINT All three methods consider the time value of money, assuming the discounted payback method is used. They are known as discounted cash flow (DCF) techniques.

The payback period

DEFINITION **The payback technique** considers the time a project will take to pay back the money invested in it. It is based on expected cash flows. To use the payback technique a company must set a target payback period.

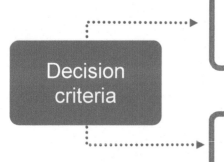

Compare the payback period to the company's target return time and if the payback for the project is quicker the project should be accepted.

It is important to understand how decisions can be made when presented with calculations.

Faced with mutually exclusive projects choose the project with the quickest payback.

KEY POINT The formula to calculate the payback period with constant annual cash flows is:

Payback period = <u>Initial investment</u>

Annual cash inflow

A payback period may not be for an exact number of years. To calculate the payback in years and months you should multiply the decimal fraction of a year by 12 to get the number of months.

When cash flows are uneven the payback has to be calculated by working out the cumulative cash flow over the life of a project.

Advantages	Disadvantages
Simple to understand.	Is not a measure of absolute profitability.
Payback is a simple measure of risk –a project with a long payback period tends to be riskier than one with a short payback period.	Ignores the time value of money.
Uses cash flows, not subjective accounting profits.	
Emphasises the cash flows in the earlier years.	Does not take into account cash flows beyond the payback period.
Firms selecting projects on the basis of payback periods may avoid liquidity problems.	

A discounted payback period may be calculated to overcome this problem.

Discounted payback

KEY POINT The discounted payback measures the time required for the present values of the net cash flows from a project to equal the present values of the cash outflows.

The discounted payback addresses the criticism of the payback period which does not take into account the time value of money.

The technique for calculating the discounted payback is identical to that of the payback period but the present value of the cash flow is calculated before calculating the cumulative cash flow.

Net present value (NPV)

A positive NPV represents the surplus funds earned on a project. This means that it tells us the impact on shareholder wealth.

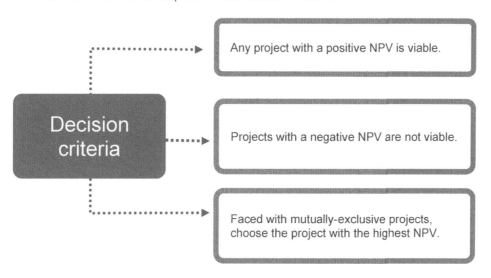

Advantages	Disadvantages
Considers the time value of money.	Fairly complex.
It is a measure of absolute profitability.	Not well understood by non-financial managers.
Considers cash flows.	It may be difficult to determine the cost of capital.
It considers the whole life of the project.	
A company selecting projects on the basis of NPV maximisation should maximise shareholders wealth.	

Internal rate of return (IRR)

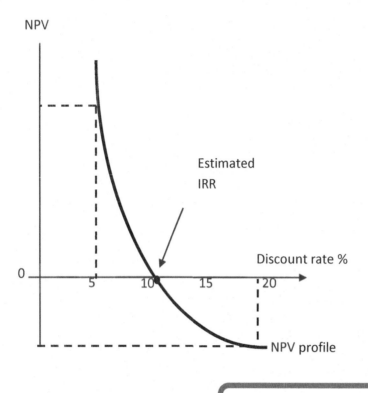

NPV

Estimated
IRR

Discount rate %

0

5   10   15   20

NPV profile

```
                          If the IRR is greater than the company's cost
               ·········▶ of capital the project should be accepted.
               :
  ┌──────────┐ :
  │          │ :                                              The IRR should
  │ Decision │ :                                              exceed the cost of
  │ criteria │ :                                              capital to be
  │          │ :                                              accepted. The higher
  └──────────┘ :                                              the IRR the better.
               :
               :          Faced with mutually-exclusive projects
               ·········▶ choose the project with the higher IRR.
```

Calculating the IRR (using linear interpolation)

The steps in linear interpolation are:

Calculate two NPVs for the project at two different costs of capital.

Use the formula to find the IRR.

KEY POINT The formula to calculate IRR:

$$IRR = L + \frac{N_L}{N_L - N_H} (H - L)$$

L = lower discount rate

H = higher discount rate

NL = NPV at the lower discount rate

NH = NPV at the higher discount rate.

Learn the formula and
ensure you can use it
for calculations!

Advantages	Disadvantages
Considers the time value of money.	It is not a measure of absolute profitability.
It is a percentage so should be easily understood by non-financial managers.	Interpolation only provides an estimate of the true IRR.
Considers cash flows.	Fairly complicated to calculate, although spreadsheets now have built-in programs.
It considers the whole life of the project.	The IRR of projects may conflict with the NPV. If this occurs the NPV must take precedence.
It can be calculated without reference to the cost of capital.	
A company selecting projects where the IRR exceeds the cost of capital should increase shareholders' wealth.	

Annuities

DEFINITION An **annuity** is a constant annual cash flow for a number of years.

If a project has equal annual cash flows, the discounted cash flow can be calculated in a quicker way.

DEFINITION The **annuity factor (AF)** is the name given to the sum of the individual discount factors (also referred to as the cumulative discount factor).

When a project has equal annual cash flows for a number of years the annuity factor may be used to discount the cash flows.

KEY POINT The formula to calculate the present value of an annuity:

PV = Annual cash flow × annuity factor (AF)

The annuity factor can be looked up on the annuity (cumulative present value) table or found using an annuity formula.

> The annuity factor tables are provided in the examination.

KEY POINT The formula to calculate the annuity factor:

$$\text{Annuity factor} = \frac{1-(1+r)^{-n}}{r}$$

Perpetuities

DEFINITION A **perpetuity** is an annual cash flow that occurs forever.

While an annuity is a constant annual cash flow for a set number of years, a perpetuity is a constant annual cash flow which continues indefinitely. It is often described as a cash flow continuing 'for the foreseeable future'.

> In the examination it may be referred to as a cash flow continuing for the foreseeable future.

Calculating the NPV of a project with a perpetuity

KEY POINT The PV of a perpetuity is found with the formula:

PV = $\dfrac{\text{Cashflow}}{r}$

or

PV = Cashflow × 1/r

1/r is known as the perpetuity factor.

Calculating the IRR of a project with a perpetuity

KEY POINT

IRR of a perpetuity = $\dfrac{\text{Annual inflow}}{\text{Initial investment}}$ × 100

Do you understand?

1. A company's cost of capital is 15% and the IRR of a project has been calculated as 10% - should this project be accepted?

2. What is an annuity factor?

3. A criticism of the payback period is that it does not consider the time value of money. How can this be addressed?

4. Ted would like to have $250 in 8 years' time. If the account he intends to make an investment in pays a rate of interest of 12% per annum, how much should be invested? Extract from present value table gives a discount rate of 0.404 (12% 8 years).

1. No – the IRR is less than the cost of capital and so the project should be rejected.
2. An annuity factor is the sum of the individual discount factors. It may also be referred to as the cumulative discount factor.
3. The discounted payback method can be used as it measures the time required for the present values of the net cash flows from a project to equal the present values of the cash outflows.
4. X = 250 × 0.404 = $101

1   The details of an investment project are as follows:

Cost of asset bought at the start of the project	$80,000
Annual cash inflow	$25,000
Cost of capital	5% each year
Life of the project	8 years

What is the present value of the project?

A   −$120,000

B $120,000

C $81,575

D   −$81,575

2   An education authority is considering the implementation of a CCTV (closed circuit television) security system in one of its schools. Details of the proposed project are as follows:

Life of project	5 years
Initial cost	$75,000
Annual savings:	
Labour costs	$20,000
Other costs	$5,000
NPV at 15%	$8,800

What is the internal rate of return for this project?

A   16%

B   18%

C   20%

D   22%

3   The following measures have been calculated to appraise a proposed project:

The internal rate of return is 12%

The return on capital employed is 16%

The payback period is 4 years

Which of the following statements is correct?

A   the payback is less than 5 years so the project should go ahead

B   the IRR is lower than the return on capital employed so the project should not go ahead

C   the IRR is greater than the cost of capital so the project should go ahead

D   The IRR is positive so the project should go ahead

15 Standard costing

The following topics are covered in this chapter:
- An introduction to standard costing
- Variance analysis
- Sales, materials cost, labour cost variances
- Variable and fixed overhead variances
- Operating statements
- Reporting of variances

15.1 AN INTRODUCTION TO STANDARD COSTING

LEARNING SUMMARY

After studying this section you should be able to:

- define what a standard cost is
- outline the different types of standard costs
- present standard costs on a standard cost card.

DEFINITION   **A standard cost** is the planned unit cost of a product or service. It is an indication of what a unit of product or service should cost.

Types of standard costs

Basic standards	Set for the long term and remain unchanged over a period of years. Often retained as a minimum standard and can be used for long term comparisons of performance.
Ideal standards	No allowance for inefficiencies such as losses or machine downtime. Almost always result in adverse variances. Can be demotivating for managers.
Attainable standards	Assume efficient levels of operation, but which include allowances for factors such as losses, waste and machine downtime. Adverse variances will reveal whether inefficiencies have exceeded this unavoidable amount.
Current standards	Based on current levels of efficiency in terms of allowances for breakdowns, wastage, losses and so on.

Standard costs per unit

The preparation of a budget requires a calculation of expected cost per unit. A standard cost can be based on absorption or marginal costing. Once standard costs for a product or service have been set, they are presented in a standard cost card:

	$
Direct materials: 10 kg @ $5	50
Direct labour: 12 hours @ $11	132
	———
Prime cost	182
Variable production overhead: 12 hours @ $9	108
	———
Variable production cost	290
	———

For each of the variable costs, the standard amount and the standard price are given.

Direct material:	standard quantity (10kg) × standard price ($5 per kg)
Direct labour	standard hours (12 hours) × standard rate ($11 per hour)
Variable production overheads	standard hours (12 hours) × standard rate ($9 per hour)

KEY POINT The standard hours for labour and overheads are usually the same as it is normally assumed that variable overheads are absorbed on the basis of labour hours.

15.2 VARIANCE ANALYSIS

LEARNING SUMMARY

After studying this section you should be able to:

- define what favourable and adverse variances.

DEFINITION A variance is the difference between actual results and the budget or standard.

- **Favourable (F) variance** – when actual results are better than expected results.

- **Adverse (A) variance** – when actual results are worse than expected results.

15.3 SALES, MATERIALS COST AND LABOUR COST VARIANCES

LEARNING SUMMARY

After studying this section you should be able to:

- outline how sales variances occur and how they are calculated
- outline how materials cost variances occur and how they are calculated
- outline how labour cost variances occur and how they are calculated.

Sales variances

Sales variances can be due to a difference in selling price and selling volume.

Sales volume variance

DEFINITION The **sales volume variance** calculates the effect on profit of the actual sales volume being different from that budgeted.

KEY POINT The sales volume variance is calculated as:

(Actual quantity sold – Budget quantity sold) × Standard margin

The standard margin is the standard contribution per unit (marginal costing), or the standard profit per unit (absorption costing).

Sales price variance

DEFINITION The **sales price variance** shows the effect on profit of selling at a different price from that expected.

KEY POINT The sales price variance is calculated as:

(Actual price – Budget price) × Actual quantity sold

Materials variances

Materials variances can be due to a difference in purchase price and quantity used.

Materials total variance

DEFINITION The **materials total variance** is the difference between the actual cost of direct material and the standard material cost of the actual production (flexed budget).

The total variance can be analysed into a materials price variance and a materials usage variance.

Materials price variance

DEFINITION The **materials price variance** analyses whether the company paid more or less than expected for the materials purchased.

Materials usage variance

Labour cost variances

Labour cost variances can be due to a difference in rate paid and hours worked.

The total variance can be analysed into a labour rate variance and a labour efficiency variance.

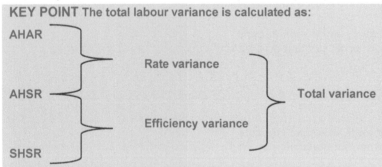

If there is idle time, the rate variance is based on the hours actually paid whilst the efficiency variance is based on the hours actually worked.

15.4 VARIABLE AND FIXED OVERHEAD VARIANCES

LEARNING SUMMARY

After studying this section you should be able to:

* outline how variable overhead variances occur and how they are calculated

* outline how fixed overhead variances occur and how they are calculated.

Variable overhead variance

Variable overhead variances are very similar to those for materials and labour because, like these direct costs, the variable overhead cost also changes when activity levels change. It is normally assumed that variable overheads vary with direct labour hours of input and the variable overhead total variance will therefore be due to expenditure or efficiency variances.

An expenditure variance arises if the variable overhead cost per hour was different to that expected.

An efficiency variance arises if working more or less hours than expected for the actual production

KEY POINT The variable overhead variance is calculated as:

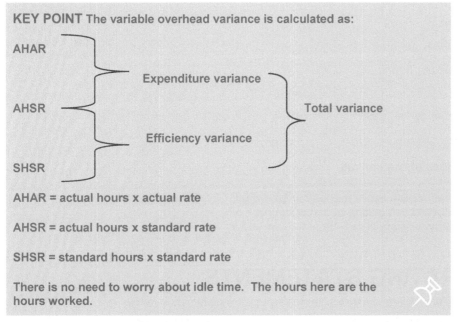

AHAR = actual hours x actual rate

AHSR = actual hours x standard rate

SHSR = standard hours x standard rate

There is no need to worry about idle time. The hours here are the hours worked.

Fixed overhead variance

DEFINITION **Fixed overhead variances** show the effect on profit of differences between actual and expected fixed overheads.

Actual and expected fixed overheads should not change when there is a change in the level of activity, consequently many of the variances calculated are based upon budgets. However, the effect on profit depends upon whether a marginal or absorption costing system is being used.

KEY POINT The expenditure variance for fixed overheads is calculated as:

= budgeted fixed cost – actual fixed cost.

This is applicable in both marginal costing and absorption costing systems.

> Did the fixed overhead cost more/less than expected?

If fixed overheads are absorbed based on hours then the volume variance can be split into capacity and efficiency:

Capacity variance	$	Did employees work more/less hours than expected?
Actual hours × FOAR per hour	X	
Less: Budgeted expenditure	Y	
	———	
Fixed overhead capacity variance	X – Y	
	———	

Efficiency variance	$	Did employees work faster/slower than expected?
Standard hours × FOAR per hour	X	
Actual hours × FOAR per hour	Y	
	———	
Fixed overhead efficiency variance	X – Y	
	———	

FOAR = fixed overhead absorption rate

15.5 OPERATING STATEMENTS

LEARNING SUMMARY

After studying this section you should be able to:

- prepare absorption costing operating statements
- prepare marginal costing operating statements.

Variances are often summarised in an operating statement. The statement allows for budgeted values to be reconciled with actual values.

If the statement starts with budgeted profit (absorption costing) or possibly budgeted contribution (marginal costing) then:

- Add the favourable variances as they increase profit/contribution
- Subtract the adverse variances as they decrease profit/contribution.

Absorption costing operating statements

	$	$	$
Budgeted profit			
Sales variances:	**Favourable**	**Adverse**	
Sale price variance			
Sales profit volume variance			
Actual sales minus the standard full cost of sales			
Cost variances:			
Material price			
Material usage			
Labour rate			
Idle time			
Labour efficiency			
Variable overhead expenditure			
Variable overhead efficiency			
Fixed overhead expenditure			
Fixed overhead capacity			
Fixed overhead efficiency			
Total variances			
Actual profit			

Marginal costing operating statements

	$	$	$
Budgeted profit			
Add: Budgeted fixed overheads			
Budgeted contribution			
Sales variances:	**Favourable**	**Adverse**	
Sales price variance			
Sales contribution volume variance			
Actual sales minus the standard marginal cost of sales			
Cost variances			
Material price			
Material usage			
Labour rate			
Idle time			
Labour efficiency			
Variable overhead expenditure			
Variable overhead efficiency			
Total of variable cost variances			
Actual contribution			
Budgeted fixed overhead			
Fixed overhead expenditure			
Actual fixed cost			
Actual profit			

15.6 REPORTING OF VARIANCES

LEARNING SUMMARY

After studying this section you should be able to:

- outline the causes of variances
- understand what factors to consider when investigating variances
- identify problems of using standard costing in modern environments.

Causes of variances

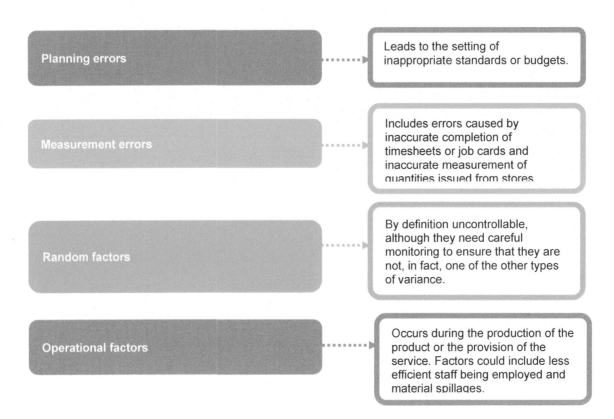

Planning errors .... Leads to the setting of inappropriate standards or budgets.

Measurement errors .... Includes errors caused by inaccurate completion of timesheets or job cards and inaccurate measurement of quantities issued from stores.

Random factors .... By definition uncontrollable, although they need careful monitoring to ensure that they are not, in fact, one of the other types of variance.

Operational factors .... Occurs during the production of the product or the provision of the service. Factors could include less efficient staff being employed and material spillages.

Factors to consider when investigating variances

The size/significance of the variance.

Whether favourable or adverse – firms often treat adverse variances as more important than favourable.

Correction costs versus benefits.

Ability to correct.

Budget reliability.

Past pattern.

Reliability of measurement and recording systems.

Problems of using standard costing in modern environments

| Products are non-standard. |
| Standard costs become outdated quickly. |
| Production is highly automated. |
| Ideal standard used in modern environments. |
| Emphasis on continuous improvement. |
| Detailed information is required. |
| Variance analysis provides results 'too late'. |

Do you understand?

1   Explain what is meant by standard costing.

2   Describe four types of standard.

3   What would an adverse materials price variance and a favourable materials usage variance indicate and what might this be caused by?

4   Explain briefly the possible causes of

   (i)   A favourable material usage variance

   (ii) A favourable labour rate variance

   (iii) An adverse sales volume contribution variance.

---

1   Standard costing is a control technique which compares standard costs and revenues with actual results to obtain variances which are used to improve performance.

2   Types of standard

   (i)   A *basic standard* is a standard established for use over a long period from which a current standard can be developed.

   (ii) An *ideal standard* is one which can be attained under the most favourable conditions, with no allowance for normal losses, waste or idle time.

   (iii) An *attainable standard* is one which can be attained if a standard unit of work is carried out efficiently. Allowances are made for normal losses.

   (iv) A *current standard* is based on current levels of performance. Allowances are made for current levels of loss and idle time, etc.

3   An adverse materials price variance and a favourable materials usage variance indicates that there is an inverse relationship between the two. This might be caused by purchasing higher quality material.

4   (i)   The material usage variance, being favourable indicates that the amount of material used was less than expected for the actual output achieved. This could be caused by the purchase of higher quality materials, which resulted in less wastage than normal.

   (ii) The labour rate variance, being favourable, indicates that the hourly wage rate paid was lower than expected. This could be due to employing a lower grade employee than was anticipated in the budget.

   (iii) The sales volume contribution variance, being adverse, indicates that the number of units sold was less than budgeted. This may have been caused by an increased sales price which has reduced customer demand, or due to the actions of competitors.

1   **What are performance standards that allow for efficient but not perfect operating conditions known as?**

   A   ideal standards

   B   current standards

   C   basic standards

   D   attainable standards

2   The following information relates to labour costs for the past month:

Budget	Labour rate	$10 per hour
	Production time	15,000 hours
	Time per unit	3 hours
	Production units	5,000 units

Actual	Wages paid	$176,000
	Production	5,500 units
	Total hours worked	14,000 hours

   There was no idle time.

   What were the labour rate and efficiency variances?

	Rate variance	Efficiency variance
A	$26,000 adverse	$25,000 favourable
B	$26,000 adverse	$10,000 favourable
C	$36,000 adverse	$2,500 favourable
D	$36,000 adverse	$25,000 favourable

3   A company is obliged to buy sub-standard materials at lower than standard price because nothing else is available.

   As an indirect result of this purchase, are the materials usage variance and labour efficiency variance likely to be adverse or favourable?

	Materials usage	Labour efficiency
A	Favourable	Favourable
B	Adverse	Favourable
C	Favourable	Adverse
D	Adverse	Adverse

4 The following is a proforma operating statement for Wick Co, a company manufacturing candles.

$

Budgeted profit

Sales volume variance _____

Standard profit on actual sales

Sales price variance _____

	Favourable ($)	Adverse ($)
Cost variances		
Materials price		
Materials usage		
Labour rate		
Labour efficiency		
Variable overhead rate		
Variable overhead efficiency		
Fixed overhead expenditure		
Fixed overhead capacity		
Fixed overhead efficiency		

Total _____

Actual profit

(a) **Which of the following THREE statements are correct?**

A   Wick Co uses standard profit per unit to calculate the sales volume variance.

B   The fixed overhead expenditure variance is the same figure as the over or under absorption of fixed overheads

C   Wick Co absorbs fixed overheads on an hourly basis.

D   The efficiency variances will all either be favourable or adverse

(b) The following information is available for Wick Co for month 1

Budgeted

Fixed overheads $20,000 to be absorbed at $10/hr
Time to make one unit   4 hours

Actual

Fixed overheads $23,000
Time taken to make 550 units   2,475 hours

Required:

Calculate the fixed overhead:

(i) **Expenditure variance and state if it is favourable or adverse**

(ii) **Capacity variance and state if it is favourable or adverse.**

(iii) **Efficiency variance and state if it is favourable or adverse.**

(c) **Is the following statement true/false?**

'A favourable fixed overhead capacity variance is likely to arise if a new machine is bought to replace an unreliable one.'

A   True

B   False

The following topics are covered in this chapter:

- Performance measurement
- Financial performance measures
- Non-financial performance indicators

16.1 PERFORMANCE MEASURMENT

LEARNING SUMMARY

After studying this section you should be able to:

- understand the purpose of performance measurement
- identify external factors affecting performance measurement
- outline what critical success factors are and how they are determined.

Performance measurement

DEFINITION **Performance measurement** is the monitoring of budgets or targets against actual results to establish how well the business and its employees are functioning as a whole and as individuals.

KEY POINT Objectives and goals of a business will vary depending on the type of business that is being operated.

- **A profit seeking company's** overall goal will be to maximise their shareholders wealth so they will want to monitor profitability (based on increasing sales and reducing costs) and growth or market share compared to competitors.

- **A not for profit organisation**, for example a government department, will want to provide the best service possible for the lowest cost so that the residents being cared for achieve value for money from the taxes they pay.

A mission statement which describes the overall goal of the organisation can be used as a guide for producing performance measures for the business.

The different elements of the mission statement can be used as a guide for producing performance measures for the business.

Purpose	Is the business meeting its main aims?
	Maximisation of shareholder wealth?
	Maintaining customer satisfaction?
	Producing innovative products/services?
Strategy	Is the business providing the products and services it planned to?
	Is the product or service being provided in the manner it intended?
Policies and culture	Are the staff behaving in the manner expected of them?
	Is customer service at an appropriate level?
Values	Are the core principles of the business being maintained and not compromised?
	Is staff morale being maintained at a suitable level?
	What is the level of staff turnover?

Suitable measures will be drawn up in accordance with the three levels of planning:

Planning level	Examples of appropriate measures
Strategic or corporate planning – often the responsibility of the senior management and will be measured by indicators that reflect the performance of the whole organisation over the longer term.	Measurement of the overall profitability of the business and/or the return made on investing surplus cash. Return on investment (ROI), return on sales produced monthly
Tactical – often the responsibility of middle management and measures may be used that summarise the performance of a department or division, breaking the strategic plan into manageable chunks for each business unit or department	Comparison of the actual costs and revenues with the budgeted costs and revenues for each business unit or department. Actual profit compared to budget produced monthly
Operational – often concerned with the day-to-day running of the organisation and are often physical measures turning the strategic and tactical plans into the day to day running of the business.	Measurement of day to day targets such as meeting production requirements, meeting sales targets and reducing wastage, quantity of rejects, number of customer complaints produced daily.

KEY POINT Short term objectives enable the businesses to monitor progression towards the ultimate long term goal and to enable performance of employees to be measured along the way.

External factors affecting performance measurement

External factors may be an important influence on an organisation's ability to achieve objectives:

- peaks and troughs in economic and market conditions

- actions of competitors

- government can have a direct effect on the workings of a private sector organisation by introducing regulations or by having departments that monitor business activity such as

    - The Competition Act which prohibits anti-competitive agreements and any abuse of a dominant market position.

    - The Office of Fair Trading who investigates any businesses suspecting of breaching the Competition Act.

- other regulations

    - Taxation – tax on alcohol and petrol with the intention of reducing consumption

    - Subsidies – subsidies given to firms providing training for employees

    - Fines and quotas – quotas or maximums are set to limit production and if exceeded fines are imposed. For example fishing quotas are set to prevent over fishing of the seas and if a trawler brings in too much then a fine is incurred.

KEY POINT Performance measures should take account of this externally imposed limitation.

Critical success factors

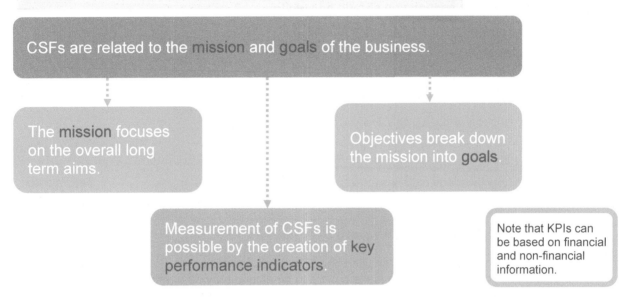

CSFs are related to the mission and goals of the business.

The mission focuses on the overall long term aims.

Objectives break down the mission into goals.

Measurement of CSFs is possible by the creation of key performance indicators.

Note that KPIs can be based on financial and non-financial information.

Examples of CSFs and KPIs	
Competitiveness	Sales growth by product or service.
	Measures of customer base.
	Relative market share and position.
Quality of service	Quality measures in every unit.
	Evaluate suppliers on the basis of quality.
	Number of customer complaints received.
	Number of new accounts lost or gained.
Customer satisfaction	Speed of response to customer needs.
	Informal listening by calling a certain number of customers each week.
	Number of customer visits to the factory or workplace.
	Number of factory and non-factory manager visits to customers.
Innovation	Proportion of new products and services to old one.
	New product or service sales levels.

16.2 FINANCIAL PERFORMANCE MEASURES

LEARNING SUMMARY

After studying this section you should be able to:

- measure profitability
- measure liquidity
- measure activity
- measure risk
- identify problems with using only financial performance measures.

KEY POINT Financial performance measures are used to monitor the inflows (revenue) and outflows (costs) and the overall management of money in the business.

Financial performance measures focus on information available from the statement of profit or loss and the statement of financial position.

Measuring profitability

The primary objective of a profit seeking company is to maximise profitability. A business needs to make a profit to be able to provide a return to any investors and to be able to grow the business by re-investment. Profitability ratios are used to monitor the achievement of this objective:

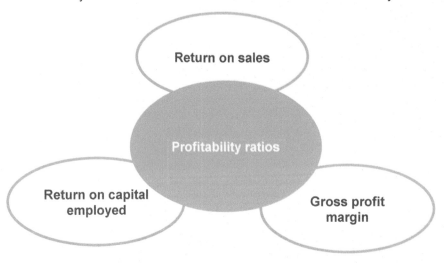

Return on capital employed

DEFINITION ROCE measures how much operating profit is generated for every $1 capital invested in the business.

It is a key measure of profitability as an investor will want to know the likely return from any investment made.

The return on capital employed % is calculated as follows:

$$\frac{\text{Operating profit}}{\text{Capital employed}} \times 100$$

A high ROCE is desirable. This can be achieved by:
- Increasing profit, e.g. through an increase in sales price or through better control of costs.
- Reducing capital employed, e.g. through the repayment of long term debt.

Either method will provide the same end answer to calculate capital employed.

Gross profit margin

DEFINITION The gross margin focuses on the trading activity of a business as it is the gross profit (revenue less cost of sales) as a percentage of revenue.

The margin works this out on an average basis across all sales for the year.

The gross profit margin % is calculated as follows:

Changes may be due to:
- selling prices
- product mix
- purchase costs
- production costs
- inventory valuations.

Return on sales (operating profit margin)

DEFINITION The **operating profit margin** is an expansion of the gross profit margin. It includes all of the items that come after gross profit but before finance charges and taxation, such as distribution and administration costs in the statement of profit or loss.

The operating profit margin % is calculated as follows:

If the gross profit margin has remained static but the operating profit margin has changed, consider the following possible causes:
- changes in employment patterns (recruitment, redundancy etc)
- changes to depreciation due to large acquisitions or disposals
- significant write-offs of irrecoverable debt
- changes in rental agreements
- significant investments in advertising
- rapidly changing fuel costs.

Measuring liquidity

A business can be profitable but at the same time encounter cash flow problems as cash at the bank and profit are not the same thing. Liquidity ratios are used to give an indication of a company's ability to manage and meet short term financial obligations.

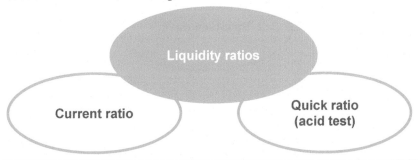

Current ratio

The current ratio is calculated as follows:

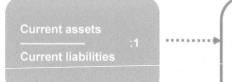

An increasingly high current ratio may appear safe but may be due to:
- high levels of inventory and receivables – indicating inventory that cannot be sold and poor credit control over receivables.
- high cash levels – indicating a loss of investment opportunities.

Quick ratio (acid test)

The quick ratio is calculated as follows:

When interpreting the quick ratio, care should be taken over the status of the bank overdraft. A business with a low quick ratio may have no issue paying amounts due if sufficient overall overdraft facilities are available.

Measuring activity

Activity ratios look at how well a business manages to convert statement of financial position items into cash. They are used to investigate how efficiently current assets are managed.

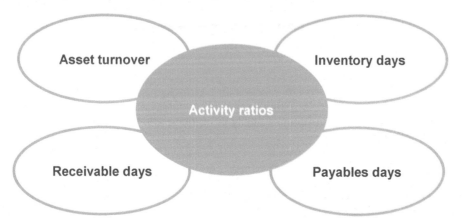

Asset turnover

Asset turnover measures how much revenue is generated from each $1 of capital employed in the business.

Asset turnover is calculated as follows:

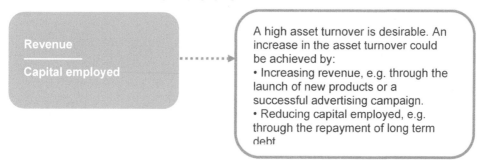

$$\frac{\text{Revenue}}{\text{Capital employed}}$$

A high asset turnover is desirable. An increase in the asset turnover could be achieved by:
• Increasing revenue, e.g. through the launch of new products or a successful advertising campaign.
• Reducing capital employed, e.g. through the repayment of long term debt

Inventory days

DEFINITION **Inventory days** indicates the average number of days that inventory items are held for before they are sold.

Inventory days is calculated as follows:

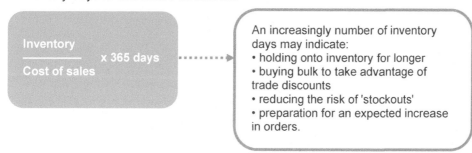

$$\frac{\text{Inventory}}{\text{Cost of sales}} \times 365 \text{ days}$$

An increasingly number of inventory days may indicate:
• holding onto inventory for longer
• buying bulk to take advantage of trade discounts
• reducing the risk of 'stockouts'
• preparation for an expected increase in orders.

Consequences of an increased inventory turnover period are the costs of storing, handling and insuring inventory levels will also increase. There is also an increased risk of inventory damage and obsolescence.

KEY POINT Year-end inventory is normally used in the calculation of inventory turnover. An average (based on the average of year-start and year-end inventories) may be used.

Receivables days

DEFINITION **Receivables days** is, on average, how long it takes to collect cash from credit customers once they have purchased goods.

It is calculated as follows:

$$\frac{\text{Trade receivables}}{\text{Credit sales}} \times 365 \text{ days}$$

Increasing receivables collection days may indicate a lack of proper credit control but can be due to:
• A significant new customer being allowed different (longer) terms.
• A deliberate policy to increase allowable credit terms to attract more trade.

KEY POINT The collection period should be compared with the stated credit policy for credit customers and previous periods' figures.

The receivables days' ratio can be distorted by a number of factors:

- using year-end figures as opposed to average receivables

- using factoring of accounts receivables figures which results in very low trade receivables

- sales on unusually long credit terms to a select few customers which is out of the norm.

Payables days

DEFINITION **Payables days** is, on average, the credit period taken by the company from its suppliers.

The payables days is calculated as follows:

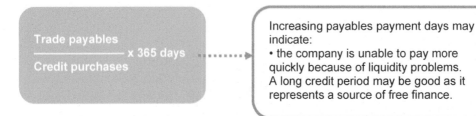

$$\frac{\text{Trade payables}}{\text{Credit purchases}} \times 365 \text{ days}$$

Increasing payables payment days may indicate:
• the company is unable to pay more quickly because of liquidity problems. A long credit period may be good as it represents a source of free finance.

KEY POINT **If the credit period is long the company may develop a poor reputation as a slow payer. Existing suppliers may decide to discontinue supplies and new suppliers may not be prepared to offer credit. Also the business may be losing out on worthwhile cash discounts for prompt payment.**

Measuring risk

It is also important for a company to manage its risk. How 'geared' a business is can be calculated to assess financial risk.

DEFINITION Gearing is the way the business is structure and financed.

Gearing indicates how well a business will be able to meet its long term debts.

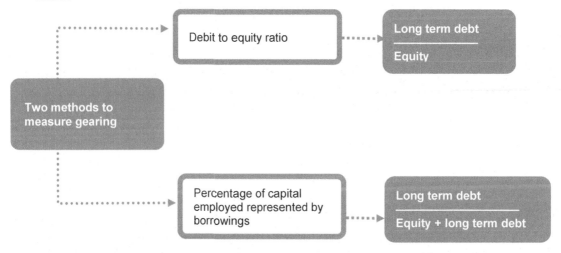

Two methods to measure gearing

Debit to equity ratio

$$\frac{\text{Long term debt}}{\text{Equity}}$$

Percentage of capital employed represented by borrowings

$$\frac{\text{Long term debt}}{\text{Equity + long term debt}}$$

KEY POINT There is no 'correct' level of gearing but if debt exceeds equity then gearing is too high.

Interest cover

Interest cover is calculated as follows:

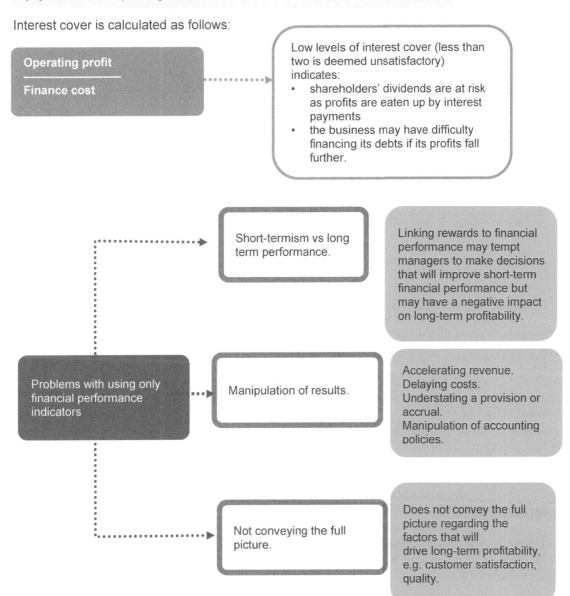

Operating profit	
Finance cost	

Low levels of interest cover (less than two is deemed unsatisfactory) indicates:
- shareholders' dividends are at risk as profits are eaten up by interest payments
- the business may have difficulty financing its debts if its profits fall further.

Short-termism vs long term performance.

Linking rewards to financial performance may tempt managers to make decisions that will improve short-term financial performance but may have a negative impact on long-term profitability.

Problems with using only financial performance indicators

Manipulation of results.

Accelerating revenue.
Delaying costs.
Understating a provision or accrual.
Manipulation of accounting policies.

Not conveying the full picture.

Does not convey the full picture regarding the factors that will drive long-term profitability, e.g. customer satisfaction, quality.

16.3 NON-FINANCIAL PERFORMANCE INDICATORS

LEARNING SUMMARY

After studying this section you should be able to:

- understand the importance of non-financial performance indicators
- measure productivity and quality.

Key performance indicators (KPIs) should not focus on profit alone. A range of performance indicators should be used and these should be a mix of financial and non-financial measures. NFPIs can be grouped together into 2 broad groups:

- **Productivity**
- **Quality**

Productivity

Productivity measures are usually given in terms of labour efficiency. However productivity measures are not restricted to labour and can also be expressed in terms of other resource inputs of the organisation such as the machine hours used for production.

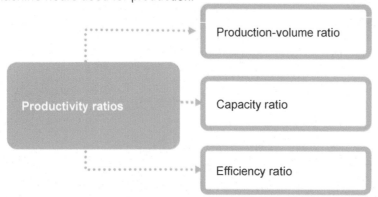

Production-volume ratio

A ratio in excess of 100% indicates that overall production is above planned levels and below 100% indicates a shortfall compared to plans. It is calculated as follows:

$$\frac{\text{Actual output measured in standard hours}}{\text{Budgeted production hours}} \times 100$$

Capacity ratio

A ratio in excess of 100% indicates that more hours have been worked than were in the budget and below 100% less hours have been worked than in the budget. It is calculated as follows:

$$\frac{\text{Actual production hours worked}}{\text{Budgeted production hours}} \times 100$$

Efficiency ratio

A ratio in excess of 100% indicates that the workforce have been more efficient than the budget predicted and below 100% less efficient than in the budget. It is calculated as follows:

$$\frac{\text{Actual output measured in standard hours}}{\text{Actual production hours worked}} \times 100$$

Quality

Quality is an issue whether manufacturing products or providing a service and targets need to be set.

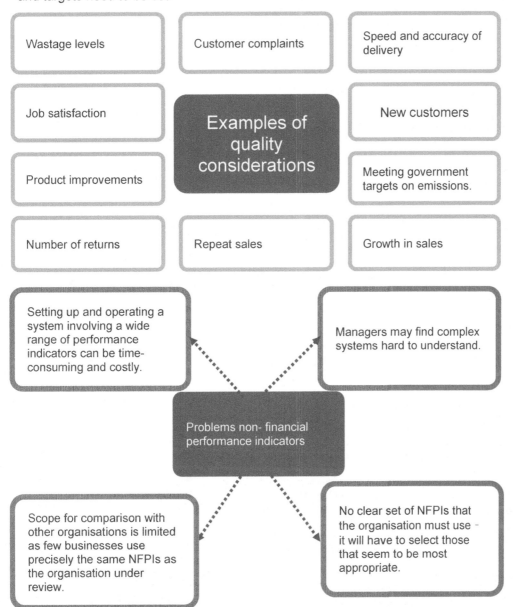

Wastage levels

Customer complaints

Speed and accuracy of delivery

Job satisfaction

Examples of quality considerations

New customers

Product improvements

Meeting government targets on emissions.

Number of returns

Repeat sales

Growth in sales

Setting up and operating a system involving a wide range of performance indicators can be time-consuming and costly.

Managers may find complex systems hard to understand.

Problems non-financial performance indicators

Scope for comparison with other organisations is limited as few businesses use precisely the same NFPIs as the organisation under review.

No clear set of NFPIs that the organisation must use – it will have to select those that seem to be most appropriate.

Balanced scorecard

The balanced scorecard was developed by Kaplan and Norton in 1993 at Harvard. It is a device for planning that enables managers to set a range of targets linked with appropriate objectives and performance measures. The framework looks at the strategy and performance of an organisation from four points of view, known in the model as four perspectives:

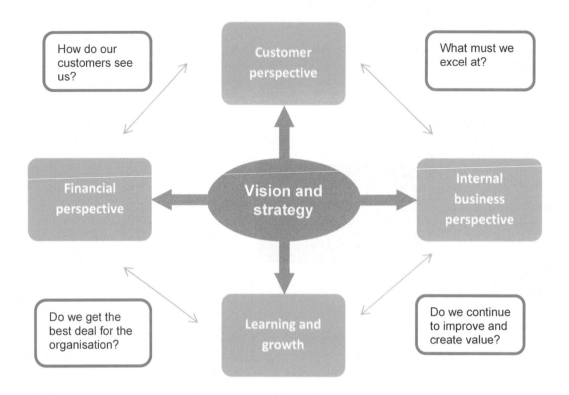

Advantages and disadvantages of the balanced scorecard

Advantages	Disadvantages
Uses four perspectives.	Large numbers of calculations required.
Less able to distort the performance measure.	Subjective.
Harder to hide bad performance.	Comparison with other businesses is not easy..
Long term rather than short term.	Arbitrary nature of arriving at the overall index of performance.
Focuses on KPIs.	
KPIs can be changed as the business changes	

Benchmarking

DEFINITION Benchmarking is the establishment, through data gathering, of targets and comparators, that permit relative levels of performance (and particular areas of underperformance) to be identified. The adoption of identified best practices should improve performance.

There are several types and levels of benchmarking, which are mainly defined by whom an organisation chooses to measure itself against.

Internal benchmarking	Other units or departments in the same organisation are used as the benchmark. Internal benchmarking is possible if the organisation is large and divided into a number of similar regional divisions. Internal benchmarking is also widely used within government.
Competitive benchmarking	The most successful competitors are used as the benchmark. Competitors are unlikely to provide willingly any information for comparison, but it might be possible to observe competitor performance (for example, how quickly a competitor processes customer orders). A competitor's product might be dismantled in order to learn about its internal design and its performance: this technique of benchmarking is called reverse engineering.
Functional benchmarking	Comparisons are made with a similar function (for example selling, order handling, despatch) in other organisations that are not direct competitors.
Strategic benchmarking	A form of competitive benchmarking aimed at reaching decisions for strategic action and organisational change. Companies in the same industry might agree to join a collaborative benchmarking process, managed by an independent third party such as a trade organisation. With this type of benchmarking, each company in the scheme submits data about their performance to the scheme organiser. The organiser calculates average performance figures for the industry as a whole from the data supplied. Each participant in the scheme is then supplied with the industry average data, which it can use to assess its own performance.

The benchmarking process

The following steps are required in a systematic benchmarking exercise:

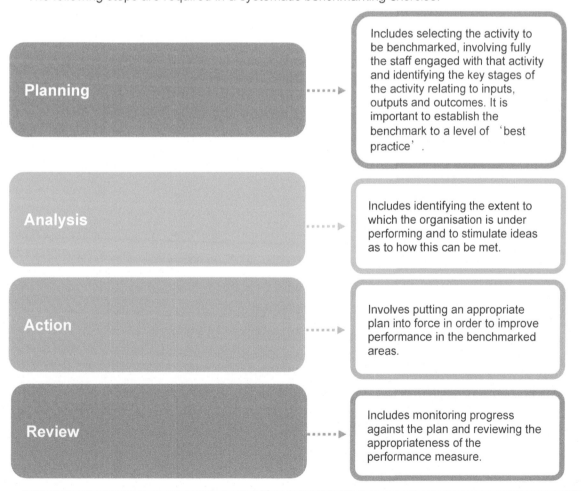

Planning ⋯⋯▷ Includes selecting the activity to be benchmarked, involving fully the staff engaged with that activity and identifying the key stages of the activity relating to inputs, outputs and outcomes. It is important to establish the benchmark to a level of 'best practice'.

Analysis ⋯⋯▷ Includes identifying the extent to which the organisation is under performing and to stimulate ideas as to how this can be met.

Action ⋯⋯▷ Involves putting an appropriate plan into force in order to improve performance in the benchmarked areas.

Review ⋯⋯▷ Includes monitoring progress against the plan and reviewing the appropriateness of the performance measure.

Do you understand?

1   What are the problems with using only financial performance indicators?

2   What are the four elements of a mission statement?

3   The capacity ratio assesses the overall production relative to the plan or budget.
    True or false?

Exam style questions

1   CAP Inc budgeted to make 50 units in July with a standard labour usage of 1.2 hours per unit. Actual output was 49 units which took 61 hours.

    What is the capacity ratio?

    A   96%

    B   98%

    C   100%

    D   102%

2   **Which of the following KPIs would be used to assess the liquidity of a company?**

    (i)   Return on capital employed

    (ii)   Gross profit percentage

    (iii)   Acid test ratio

    (iv)   Gearing ratio

    A   (i) and (ii) only

    B   (iii) only

    C   (iv) only

    D   (iii) and (iv) only

3   JKL Inc budgeted to make 1,000 units in May using 2,000 hours of direct labour. Actual output was 1,100 units which took 2,300 hours.

    What is the production/volume ratio?

    A   91%

    B   105%

    C   110%

    D   115%

4   Mal Co currently sells 25 styles of sports watches. The market has remained static with an overall revenue of $50 million.

Mal Co is always trying to bring out new designs and colours to try and increase market share or at least maintain it. In order to not fall behind their competitors, Mal Co tries to bring new products to the market quickly. Therefore Mal Co undertakes market research one year, and the results of that market research are incorporated in the new styles/colours that are launched the next year.

Historically, Mal Co have measured their performance by looking for an increase in the revenue and net profit figures and ensuring that there is cash in the bank. A new financial manager has been appointed who is keen to increase the range of performance measures used by Mal Co.

The following data is available:

	Year ended 31 October 20X3	Year ended 31 October 20X4
Revenue	$5.75 million	$6 million
Number of styles	22	25
Net profit	$345,000	$348,000
Market research costs	$200,000	$150,000

Required:

(a)   **Calculate:**

   (i)   **Net profit percentage for 20X4**

   (ii)   **Market share for 20X4**

   (iii)   **Increase in revenue**

   (iv)   **Revenue per style of watch for 20X4**

   (v)   **Increase in sales per $ of market research**

(b)   **Mal Co are considering setting up another division selling expensive watches. The two divisions would be run as profit centres, with head office costs being allocated to each division. Managers' bonuses will be dependent on the divisions meeting their targets. Targets that are being considered are:**

   (i)   **Gross profit percentage**

   (ii)   **Contribution**

   (iii)   **Net profit for the division**

   (iv)   **Return on capital employed.**

   Which of the targets should be used to assess the performance of the divisional manager and provide motivation?

   A   **(i) only**

   B   **(i) and (ii) only**

   C   **(i), (ii) and (iii) only**

   D   **All of them**

17 Performance measurement in specific situations

The following topics are covered in this chapter:

- Divisional performance measurement
- Manufacturing industries
- Service sector
- Non-profit seeking and public sector organisations
- Cost control and cost reduction

17.1 DIVISIONAL PERFORMANCE MEASURMENT

LEARNING SUMMARY

After studying this section you should be able to:

- understand how businesses can vary and the impact of this on performance measurement
- describe the difficulties of measuring the output of service providers
- outline the different types of responsibility centres and consider managerial performance
- calculate return on investment and residual income, understanding the advantages and disadvantages of each.

There are many different types of businesses in existence that can broadly be placed into one the following groups:

PUBLIC SECTOR ORGANISATION

SERVICE PROVIDER

NON-PROFIT ORGANISATION (CHARITY)

MANUFACTURING INDUSTRY

Businesses need to monitor the performance of their objectives to ensure they are able to succeed in their chosen field although each face difficulties in deciding on appropriate measures to use.

Difficulties of measuring service providers output:

- Intangible nature of the service
- The variability of the service
- Simultaneous production and consumption of the service
- Perishability of the service.

KEY POINT Non-profit and public organisations will have difficulties deciding on performance measures as the usual financial performance measures will not be applicable.

Measuring managerial performance

KEY POINT The personal performance of the manager is not the same as the overall performance of the division due to external factors which are outside of the control of the organisation.

A manager may be in control of a division which faces fierce competition and difficult operating conditions and therefore will not be able to grow the business easily. Another manager may be given a division which faces less competition and an easier business environment.

Set specific managerial objectives

Individual managers can be set specific objectives against which their performance can be measured at regular intervals. These objectives will be linked to the overall objectives of the organisation as a whole.

Use measures based on controllable costs and revenue i.e. controllable profit

Budget targets can distinguish between controllable and uncontrollable costs and revenue. The divisional performance can be measured against the total budget using traceable costs and revenues whereas managerial performance can be measured based on what the controllable element is.

The major problem is the difficulty in deciding what is controllable or traceable. If we are assessing the performance of a manager we should only consider those factors that are capable of being controlled by that manager.

Pro-forma of a controllable profit statement

	$	$
Sales:		
External	X	
Internal	X	
		X
Controllable divisional variable costs		(X)
Controllable divisional fixed costs		(X)
Controllable divisional profit		X
Other traceable divisional variable costs		(X)
Other traceable divisional fixed costs		(X)
Traceable divisional profit		X
Apportioned head office cost		(X)
Net profit		X

Responsibility centres

Responsibility centre:	Responsibilities of management:	Examples of measures to assess performance:
Cost centre	Costs only	• total cost and cost per unit • cost variances • non-financial performance indicators (NFPIs) related to quality, productivity and efficiency
Revenue centre	Revenues only	• total sales and market share • sales variances • NFPIs related to customer satisfaction
Profit centre	Costs and revenues	All the above plus: • profit percentages • working capital ratios
Investment centre	Costs, revenues, investments and disposal of assets	All of the above plus: • Return on Investment (ROI) • Residual Income (RI)

Return on investment (ROI)

DEFINITION   Return on investment (ROI) is a similar measure to ROCE but is used to appraise the investment decisions of an individual division.

$$\frac{\text{Controllable profit}}{\text{Controllable capital employed}} \times 100$$

• Controllable profit is usually taken after depreciation but before tax.
• Capital employed is total assets less current liabilities or total equity plus long term debt.
• Non-current assets might be valued at cost, net replacement cost or carrying amount. The value of assets employed could be either an average value for the period as a whole or a value as at the end of the period
• An average value for the period is preferable.

Advantages and disadvantages of ROI

Advantages	Disadvantages
Familiar and simple calculation.	Open to manipulation.
Based on accounting information.	May be distorted by inflation.
Uses readily available information.	May discourage investment in new assets.
Widely used measure.	Use of a percentage comparison can be misleading.
Gives result in percentage terms so can be used to compare business units of different sizes.	May lead to non-goal congruence.

Residual Income (RI)

RI = Controllable profit – notional interest on capital

- Controllable profit is calculated in the same way as for ROI.
- Notional interest on capital = the capital employed in the division multiplied by a notional cost of capital or interest rate.
 - Capital employed is calculated in the same way as for ROI.
 - The selected cost of capital could be the company's average cost of funds (cost of capital). However, other interest rates might be selected, such as the current cost of borrowing, or a target ROI.

Advantages and disadvantages of RI

Advantages	Disadvantages
Encourages new investment.	Not comparable with different size business units.
Interest charge.	Based on accounting measures.
Absolute measure.	Determination of the appropriate cost of capital.

17.2 MANUFACTURING INDUSTRIES

LEARNING SUMMARY

After studying this section you should be able to:

- outline the different varieties of performance indicators that exist

- outline the appropriate measures of performance for the different costing techniques that occur in manufacturing situations.

Manufacturing industries are able to use a variety of performance indicators:

- **Financial indicators** for overall profitability and liquidity of the business

- **Non-financial indicators** for productivity and quality

- **Variance analysis** for sales, materials, labour and overheads

- **Labour turnover**.

Contract costing	Contract costing is used when a job or project is large and will take a significant length of time (usually more than one accounting period) to complete. Cost control is vital and so frequent comparisons of budgeted and actual data are needed to monitor: • cost over-runs • time over-runs. • ratio of cost incurred to value of work certified • amount of remedial work subsequently required. • levels of idle time • amounts of wasted material • inventory levels • utilisation of plant. The level of profit being earned on the contract can be checked as each architect or quantity surveyor's certificate is received.
Job costing	Job costing is used to cost individual, unique jobs. Job costing is contract costing on a smaller scale both in value and time therefore many of the performance measures will be identical. The type of firm that is using job costing will influence the type of measure used. For example; practising accountants may use a ratio of chargeable time for a job to total time required to complete the job; garages may use average age of inventories of spares and printers may use cost per printed page.
Process costing	Process costing is used when manufacturing consists of a sequence of continuous operations or processes. Measures include: • levels of abnormal loss • levels of rejected production • production time. Inventory levels and cost targets would be monitored as well as any bottlenecks identified and cured.
Batch costing	Being a 'half-way house' between job and process costing, performance measures used in those two systems may be equally appropriate for batch costing.

17.3 SERVICE SECTOR

LEARNING SUMMARY

After studying this section you should be able to:

- identify a variety of financial performance indicators that may be used for the service sector

- identify a variety of quality considerations appropriate for the service sector.

The service sector consists of banks, airlines, transport companies, accountancy and consultancy firms and service shops.

Main aspects of performance related to service organisations:

Financial performance

Service quality

Financial performance

Typical ratios that could be used by a service organisation include:

- revenue per 'service'
- revenue per 'principal' or partner in, for example, a management consultancy
- staff costs as a % of revenue
- space costs as a % of revenue
- training costs as a % of revenue
- profit %
- current ratio
- quick asset ratio
- market share
- market share increase year by year.

These financial indicators are not exhaustive and are intended to provide and idea as to how performance may be assessed within the service sector.

KEY POINT Financial ratio analysis is of use but due to the 'human' nature of a service provider, the quality of the service also needs to be considered.

Service quality

Quality is seen to be a particularly important non-financial performance indicator in the service sector.

Reliability	Access	Aesthetics
Responsiveness	**Examples of quality considerations**	Availability
Courtesy		Cleanliness
Competence	Communications	Comfort

These are examples of quality considerations; others may be used within different scenarios.

17.4 NON-PROFIT SEEKING AND PUBLIC SECTOR ORGANISATIONS

LEARNING SUMMARY

After studying this section you should be able to:

- outline the value for money (VFM) concept
- understand how to calculate the performance indicators of economy, efficiency and effectiveness.

Two main problems involved in assessing performance of these organisations:

* the problem of identifying and measuring objectives

* the problem of identifying and measuring outputs

Objectives

Performance indicators can be devised that indicate the extent to which such objectives have been achieved.

Although the detail will vary depending on the organisation involved, we could suggest that the general objective of non-profit seeking organisations is to provide the best possible service within a limited resource budget.

KEY POINT Outputs of organisations in these sectors are often not valued in money terms so the issue arises as to how we measure the output.

Value for Money (VFM)

The value for money (VFM) concept has been developed as a useful means of assessing performance in an organisation which is not seeking profit.

VFM concept revolves around the 3Es:

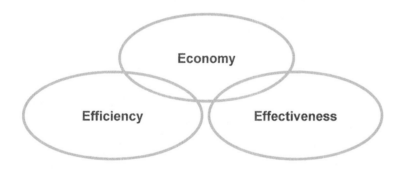

* **Economy** (an input measure) – measures the relationship between money spent and the inputs. Are the resources used the cheapest possible for the quality required?

* **Efficiency** (link inputs with outputs) – is the maximum output being achieved from the resources used?

* **Effectiveness** (links outputs with objectives) – to what extent the outputs generated achieve the objectives of the organisation.

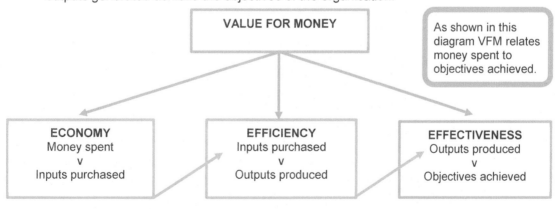

KEY POINT VFM relates money spent to objectives achieved, focused on financial performance. Non-profit seeking organisations will also need to consider non-financial performance, particularly quality.

Calculations for economy, efficiency and effectiveness:

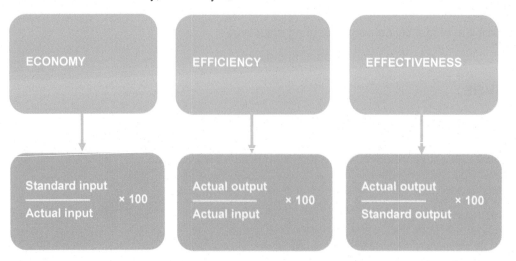

ECONOMY	EFFICIENCY	EFFECTIVENESS

$$\frac{\text{Standard input}}{\text{Actual input}} \times 100 \qquad \frac{\text{Actual output}}{\text{Actual input}} \times 100 \qquad \frac{\text{Actual output}}{\text{Standard output}} \times 100$$

It is important that calculations can be applied to scenarios and the results are understood.

17.5 COST CONTROL AND COST REDUCTION

LEARNING SUMMARY

After studying this section you should be able to:

- compare cost control and cost reduction
- describe and evaluate cost reduction methods including value analysis.

Cost control

DEFINITION **Cost control** involves the setting of targets for cost centre managers and then monitoring performance against those targets. Performance can be measured using standard costing and variance analysis.

DEFINITION **Cost reduction** is the reduction in unit cost of goods or services without impairing suitability for the use intended i.e. without reducing value to the customer.

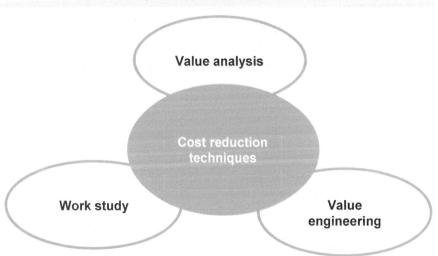

Value analysis

In other words, value analysis is improving profitability by reducing costs without necessarily increasing prices.

One of the problems with value analysis is placing a meaning on the word 'value'. It is useful to distinguish two types of value:

- **Utility value** is the value an item has because of the uses to which it can be put.

- **Esteem value** is the value put on an item because of its beauty, craftsmanship, etc.

The value analysis method	
Step 1	Establish the precise requirements of the customer.
Step 2	Establish and evaluate alternative ways of achieving the requirements of the customers. (i) Materials – amount required, acceptable level of wastage (can it be improved?), alternative, cheaper materials. (ii) Labour – can the cost be reduced by eliminating operations or changing production methods? (iii) Other factors – can new, cheaper processes be found? Would a cheaper finish be acceptable?
Step 3	Authorise any proposals put forward as a result of step 2.
Step 4	Implementation of proposals.
Step 5	Evaluate feedback from new proposals to establish the benefits from the change.

Benefits of value analysis:

- good impressions shown in their requirements and this will lead to increased sales

- attract better staff, due both to the prospects for an outlet for their ideas and the higher morale resulting from the team approach

- economic and financial benefits arising from the elimination of unnecessary complexity and the better use of resources.

Value engineering

Work study

DEFINITION **Work study** is a systematic examination of the methods of carrying out activities in order to improve the effective use of resources and to set up standards of performance for the activities carried out.

Two areas of work study:

- **Method study** – the analysis of current and new work methods to enable more effective techniques to be used and to reduce costs.

- **Work measurement** – identifying the time it should take to complete a specific task by an experienced and qualified member of staff.

Objectives of work study:

Analyse the present method of doing a job, systematically in order to develop a new and better method.

Measure the work content of a job by measuring the time required to do the job for a qualified worker and hence to establish standard time.

Increase the productivity by ensuring the best possible use of human, machine and material resources and to achieve best quality product/service at minimum possible cost.

Improve operational efficiency.

Control reports

General criteria for control reports:

Relevant to the information needs of their recipients.

Linked to responsibility.

Timely and reliable.

Designed to communicate effectively.

Cost-effective.

Do you understand?

1   A government body uses measures based upon the 'three Es' to the measure value for money generated by a publicly funded hospital. It considers the most important performance measure to be 'cost per successfully treated patient'.

   Which of the three E's best describes the above measure?

   A   Economy

   B   Effectiveness

   C   Efficiency

   D   Externality

2   Which of the following measures would not be appropriate for a cost centre?

   A   Cost per unit

   B   Contribution per unit

   C   Comparison of actual labour cost to budget labour cost

   D   Under or over absorption of overheads

3   How is residual income calculated?

4   Name the three cost reduction techniques.

1   C
   Cost per patient is a measure of output related to input

2   B
   Contribution is calculated as sales revenue less variable costs. The manager of a cost centre will not be responsible for the revenue therefore this is not an appropriate measure.

3   RI = Controllable profit – notional interest on capital

4   Value analysis, work study and value engineering.

1   A government is looking at assessing state schools by reference to a range of both financial and non-financial factors, one of which is average class sizes.

    Which of the three E's best describes the above measure?

    A   Economy

    B   Effectiveness

    C   Efficiency

    D   Externality

2   RL Inc budgeted to make 200 units in June with a standard labour usage of 0.6 hours per unit. Actual output was 180 units which took 126 hours.

    What is the efficiency ratio?

    A   86%

    B   90%

    C   105%

    D   116%

3   In the last year a division's controllable return on investment was 25% and its controllable profit was $80,000. The cost of finance appropriate to the division was 18% per annum.

    What was the division's controllable residual income in the last year?

    A $5,600

    B $22,400

    C $74,400

    D $76,400

18 Spreadsheets

The following topics are covered in this chapter:
- Uses of spreadsheets
- Advantages and disadvantages of spreadsheets

18.1 USES OF SPREADSHEETS

LEARNING SUMMARY

After studying this section you should be able to:

- understand the uses of spreadsheets in the workplace
- outline how to enter a formulae
- recall examples of statistical functions.

DEFINITION   A spreadsheet is a computer package that is used to manipulate data.

One of the most useful functions of a spreadsheet is being able to input formulae to enable calculation to happen automatically when data is input in specific cells. Spreadsheets are designed to analyse data and sort list items, not for long-term storage of raw data. A spreadsheet should be used for 'crunching' numbers and storage of single list items.

Entering formulae

- A formula always starts with an equal sign (=) in Excel.
- Formulae consist of numbers, cell co-ordinates (e.g. A2, F7), operators and functions. Operators perform actions on numbers and coordinates.

Functions perform more advanced actions on numbers and coordinates.

The BODMAS (Brackets off, Division, Multiplication, Addition, Subtraction) rule must be used to evaluate an arithmetic problem:

- use brackets to clarify the correct order of operations and evaluate expressions within the brackets first
- perform division and multiplication before addition and subtraction
- work from left to right if the expression contains only addition and subtraction.

> Examples of operators are plus, minus, divide and multiply.

Steps to enter formulae

Select the cell where you want to enter the formula.
Press the equal sign (=) on the keyboard (or click on the sign in the formula bar, if one is shown).
Key in the formula directly from the keyboard or use the mouse to select the cells you want in the formula. There are no spaces in a formula.
Press the <Enter> key.
When you have entered a formula, the resulting value appears in that cell. The formula is only visible in the formula bar.

> Questions testing this syllabus area often present a scenario which requires an appropriate formula to be identified.

Statistical functions

SUM	the total of the values in the list
AVG	the average of the values in the list
MAX	the highest value in the list
MIN	the lowest value in the list.

Using spreadsheets in the workplace

Spreadsheets are a convenient way of setting up all sorts of charts, records and tables. Uses include:

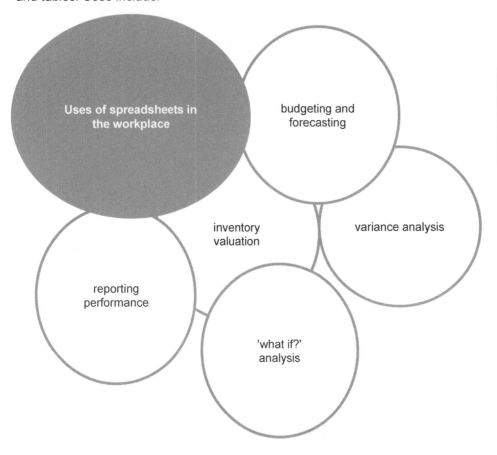

Ensure you are familiar with the different uses of spreadsheets – examples may be drawn upon in the examination.

18.2 ADVANTAGES AND DISADVANTAGES OF SPREADSHEETS

LEARNING SUMMARY

After studying this section you should be able to:

• outline the advantages and disadvantages of spreadsheets.

Advantages and disadvantages

Advantages	Disadvantages
Spreadsheet programs are relatively easy to use.	Data must be recopied over and over again to maintain it in separate data files.
Spreadsheet functions enable data to be processed more quickly.	Spreadsheets are not able to identify data input errors.
Spreadsheets are often easier to read than hand written tables.	Spreadsheets lack detailed sorting and querying abilities.
They include graphing functions that allow for quick reporting and analysis of data.	There can be sharing violations among users wishing to view or change data at the same time.
	Spreadsheets are restricted to a finite number of records.
They should reduce calculation errors.	Spreadsheets are open to cyber-attack through viruses, hackers and general system failure.

Do you understand?

1   What do the following statistical functions do?

   (i)   SUM

   (ii)   AVG

   (iii) MIN

2   State two advantages of using spreadsheets.

1 **Which TWO of the following statements are true in relation to spreadsheets?**

    A   A spreadsheet consists of records and files.

    B   Most spreadsheets have a facility to allow data within them to be displayed graphically.

    C   A spreadsheet could be used to prepare a budgeted statement of profit or loss.

    D   A spreadsheet is the most suitable software for storing large volumes of data.

2 **Which of the following are advantages of spreadsheet software over manual approaches?**

    (i)   Security

    (ii)   Speed

    (iii)   Accuracy

    (iv)   Legibility

    A   All of them

    B   (ii), (iii) and (iv)

    C   (ii) and (iv)

    D   (i) and (iv)

3 A company manufactures a single product. In a computer spreadsheet the cells F1 to F12 contain the budgeted monthly sales units for the 12 months of next year in sequence with January sales in cell F1 and finishing with December sales in F12. The company policy is for the closing inventory of finished goods each month to be 10% of the budgeted sales units for the following month.

Which of the following formulae will generate the budgeted production (in units) for March next year?

    A   = [F3 + (0.1*F4)]

    B   = [F3 – (0.1*F4)]

    C   = [(1.1*F3) – (0.1*F4)]

    D   = [(0.9*F3) + (0.1*F4)]

Answers to exam style questions

CHAPTER 1

1   C

The manager of a profit centre needs to know about the profits of the centre, i.e. revenues and costs. Revenues are only appropriate for a revenue centre; costs for a cost centre; and revenues, costs and assets employed for an investment centre.

2   B

Cost accounting is not part of financial accounting.

3   A

Emily is only responsible for costs.

CHAPTER 2

1   C

This is the definition of systematic sampling.

2   B

Simple random sampling always eliminates selection bias but does not guarantee a representative sample.

3   B

Secondary data is used for one purpose, although it was originally collected for another purpose.

CHAPTER 3

1   D

A simple bar chart would show five bars illustrating the different salaries in different regions.

2   63°

241/1,384 × 360 = 62.69° = 63°

3   D

CHAPTER 4

1

Cost	Fixed	Variable	Semi-variable
Director's salary	✓		
Wood		✓	
Rent of factory	✓		
Phone bill – includes a line rental			✓
Factory workers wage		✓	

2   C

Use the two levels of production above 1,100 units per month for the high-low analysis as at these levels fixed costs are the same.

Units	Total cost ($)
1,400	68,200
1,200	66,600
200	1,600

Variable cost per unit = ($1,600 ÷ 200) = $8

Total fixed cost (above 1,100 units) = [$68,200 – (1,400 × $8)] = $57,000

Total cost for 1,000 units = [($57,000 – $6,000) + (1,000 × $8)] = $59,000

3   D

Graph D is consistent with the cost behaviour for total materials given.

Graph A implies that there is a certain range of activity (just above 15,000 units) when total materials cost is constant.

Graph B implies that total materials cost falls beyond 15,000 units of activity.

Graph C implies that the lower cost per unit for materials applies only to units purchased in excess of 15,000.

CHAPTER 5

1 $4,350

{[Buffer Inventory + (EOQ ÷2)] × Annual holding cost per component}

= [700 units + (1500 units ÷ 2)] × $3.00 = $4,350

2   B

- If prices have fallen during the year, AVCO will give a higher value of closing inventory than FIFO, which values goods for resale at the latest prices.

- Where the value of closing inventory is higher, profits are higher.

3   B

	Items	Unit value $	$
Opening inventory	6	15	90
January: purchases	10	19.80	198
	16	18	288
February: sales	(10)	18	(180)
	6	18	108
March: purchases	20	24.50	490
	26	23	598
March: sales	(5)	23	(115)
	21	23	483

		$
Sales (15 × $30)		450
Cost of sales		
Opening Inventory	90	
Purchases	688	
Closing Inventory	(483)	
		(295)
Gross profit		155

CHAPTER 6

1   A

Direct labour costs are credited to wages and salaries and debited to work-in-progress.

2

Cost	Direct	Indirect
Basic pay for production workers	✓	
Supervisors wages		✓
Bonus for salesman		✓
Production workers overtime premium due to general pressures.		✓
Holiday pay for production workers		✓
Sick pay for supervisors		✓
Time spent by production workers cleaning the machinery		✓

3   **$300,000**

(4,800 units × 5 hours × $10 per hour) ÷ 0.80 = $300,000

CHAPTER 7

1 **$58,540**

Reapportion service cost centre K first as it does work for service cost centre J but not vice versa.

	G	H	J	K
Overhead cost ($)	40,000	50,000	30,000	18,000
Reapportion K	9,000	7,200	1,800	(18,000)
			31,800	
Reapportion J	9,540		(31,800)	
	$58,540			

2 **B**

	$
Actual expenditure	56,389
Absorbed cost (12,400 × 1.02 × $4.25)	53,754
Total under-absorption	2,635

3 **D**

Over-absorbed overheads increase profit, and so are recorded as a credit entry in either an over-absorbed overhead account or directly as a credit in the statement of profit and loss. The matching debit entry could be either in the WIP account or the production overhead control account, depending on the costing system used.

CHAPTER 8

1 **C**

Total variable cost	= $(4 + 5 + 3 + 3) = $15
Contribution per unit	= $20 – $15 = $5
Total contribution earned	= $5 × 800 = $4,000

2 **A**

Profit figures only differ if inventory changes in the period.

3 **12,500 units**

Absorption costing profit = $2,000 > Marginal Costing profit = $(3,000)

Therefore Production > Sales by $5,000

$5,000 = OAR × number of units change in inventory

$5,000 = $2 × number of units change in inventory

Therefore number of units change in inventory = $\dfrac{\$5,000}{\$2}$ = 2,500

If Sales = 10,000 units, therefore Production = Sales + 10,000 units = 12,500 units.

CHAPTER 9

1 **$21,150**

This can be calculated as a balancing figure in the process account.

Process account

	kg		$		kg		$
Input (balance)	3,000		21,150	Output	2,800	(× 7.50)	21,000
Abnormal gain	100	(× 7.50)	750	Normal loss	300	(× 3)	900
			———				———
			21,900				21,900
			———				———

Alternatively:

	$
Cost of output (2,800 × 7.50)	21,000
Scrap value of normal loss (300 × 3)	900
	———
	21,900
Less: Value of abnormal gain (100 × 7.50)	(750)
	———
Cost of input	21,150

2 **A**

	$
Opening WIP	1,710
Completion of opening WIP (300 × 0.40 × $10)	1,200
Units started and completed in the month	
(2,000 − 300) × $10	17,000
	———
Total value (2,000 units)	19,910
	———

3 **B**

Finished output = (20,000 + 110,000 − 40,000) = 90,000 units.

Closing WIP = 40,000 units 50% complete = 20,000 equivalent units.

Cost per equivalent unit (in $000) = $132,000/(90,000 + 20,000)

= $1,200 per equivalent unit/finished car.

CHAPTER 10

1 **D**

A charitable foundation will be a not-for-profit organisation.

2 **A and C**

Services are usually (but not always) associated with labour and labour costs, low material costs and relatively high indirect costs. Service costing also makes use of composite cost units, such as the cost per guest/day, cost per patient/day, cost per passenger/mile and so on.

3   C

A service is intangible and inventory cannot be held. Services generally have a high level of fixed costs and there are often difficulties in identifying a suitable cost unit.

CHAPTER 11

1

Cost	Internal failure costs	External failure costs	Inspection costs	Prevention costs
The costs of a customer service team		✓		
The cost of equipment maintenance				✓
The cost of operating test equipment			✓	

A customer service team deals with customer queries and complaints from outside the organisation, typically after goods have been delivered to the customer. The costs of this team arise from quality failures and are preventable. They are external failure costs. Maintenance is intended to prevent machine breakdowns and so to prevent quality failures, and they are therefore prevention costs. Test equipment is used for inspection.

2   B

	$
Sales revenue: 600 units × $450	450
Return required: 20% × $450	90
	────
Target cost per unit:	360

3   C

CHAPTER 12

1   0.69

$$b = \frac{(11 \times 13,467) - (440 \times 330)}{(11 \times 17,986) - (440)^2} = \frac{2,937}{4,246} = 0.6917 = 0.69$$

You should use the formulae provided in the examination (formulae sheet)

2   A

3   A

Quarter	'Real' sales
1	$\dfrac{109}{100} \times 100 = 109.0$
2	$\dfrac{120}{110} \times 100 = 109.1$
3	$\dfrac{132}{121} \times 100 = 109.1$
4	$\dfrac{145}{133} \times 100 = 109.0$

The 'real' series is approximately constant and keeping up with inflation.

CHAPTER 13

1   B

Flexed budget:

	Budget	Flexed budget	Actual
Sales (units)	120,000	100,000	100,000
	$000	$000	$000
Sales revenue	1,200	1,000	995
Variable printing costs	360	300	280
Variable production overheads	60	50	56
Fixed production cost	300	300	290
Fixed administration cost	360	360	364
Profit/(Loss)	120	(10)	5

2   B

	Original Budget	Flexed Budget
Sales units	1,000	1,200
	$	$
Sales revenue	100,000	120,000
Direct material	40,000	48,000
Direct labour	20,000	24,000
Variable overhead	15,000	18,000
Fixed overhead	10,000	10,000
Profit	15,000	20,000

3

(a)   Cash received in March = $15,000 × 0.5 × 0.97 + $12,000 × 0.5 = $13,275

(b)   Payment to suppliers in March = $21,000 × 0.75 + $2,000 − $3,000 = $14,750

(c)   Chain base index in February $15,000/$12,000 × 100 = 125

Chain base index in March $21,000/$15,000 × 100 = 140

(d)   Gap 1 B

Gap 2 B

CHAPTER 14

1   C

	$	AF	$
Outflow	(80,000)	1.000	(80,000)
Cash inflow $25,000 each year for 8 years	25,000	6.463	161,575
Present value of project			$81,575

2   C

Try 20%

Year	Cash	20%	PV
	$		$
0	(75,000)		(75,000)
1 – 5	25,000	2.991	74,775
			(225)

$$IRR = 15 + \frac{8,800}{(8,800 - -225)} \times 5$$

$$IRR = 15 + \frac{8,800}{9,025} \times 5$$

IRR   = 19.88% therefore 20% to the nearest 1%

3   C

Statement A is not correct as there is no company policy to confirm the payback is appropriate. Statement B is not correct as the IRR and ROCE are not comparable. Statement D is not correct as the IRR is always a positive whether the project is acceptable or not.

Statement C is correct as the IRR must be greater than the cost of capital (the discount rate) used to appraise the project as the project has a return therefore a positive NPV at the company's cost of capital so the project should go ahead.

CHAPTER 15

1   D

This is a definition of 'attainable standards'. Attainable standards are widely used in practice.

2   D

Ah × Ar =	$176,000		
	Rate variance	$36,000 A	
Ah × Sr = 14,000 hrs × $10	$140,000		
	Efficiency variance	$25,000 F	
Sh × Sr = 3 hrs × 5,500 units × $10	$165,000		

3   D

Usage of materials is likely to be adverse as the materials are sub-standard, thus there will be more wastage and a higher level of rejects.

Time spent by the labour force on rejected items that will not become output leads to higher than standard time spent per unit of output.

4   (a)   A, C and D

  (b)   (i)   The expenditure variance is $23,000 – $20,000 = $3000 and is adverse

    (ii)   The capacity variance is (2,475 hours × $10) – $20,000 = $4,750 and is favourable

    (iii) The efficiency variance is (550 units × 4 hours × $10) – (2,475 hours × $10) = $2,750 and is adverse

  (c)   A

CHAPTER 16

1   D

Actual production hours = 61 hours

Budgeted production hours = 50 × 1.2 = 60 hours

Capacity ratio = 61/60 = 1.017 or 102%

2   B

(i) and (ii) are financial indicators and (iv) is a risk indicator

3   C

Actual output in standard hours = 1,100 × 2 = 2,200 hours

Budgeted production hours = 2,000 hours

Production/volume ratio = 2,200/2,000 = 1.1 or 110%

4   (a)   Calculations

    (i)   Net profit percentage = $348,000/$6,000,000 = 5.8%

    (ii)   Market share $6,000,000/$50,000,000 = 12%

    (iii)   Increase in revenue = $0.25m/$5.75m = 4.35%

    (iv)   Revenue per style of watch = $6,000,000/25 = $240,000

    (v)   Increase in sales per $ of market research = $250,000/$200,000 = 1.25

  (b)   B – net profit for the division would include the allocated head office expenses which are not controllable, and would therefore affect motivation. ROCE is calculated using net profit so this would be misleading as well.

CHAPTER 17

1   C

Class sizes are the result of the number of pupils educated (output), the number of teachers employed (input) and how well the timetable is organised in using those teachers.

2   A

Actual output in standard hours = 180 × 0.6 = 108 hours

Actual production hours = 126 hours

Efficiency ratio = 108/126 = 0.857 or 86%

3   B

Controllable assets = 80,000 ÷ 0.25 = $320,000

RI = $80,000 − ($320,000 × 0.18) = $80,000 − $57,600 = $22,400

CHAPTER 18

1   B and C

A database (rather than a spreadsheet) contains records and files and is most suitable for storing large volumes of data.

2   B

All are said to be advantages of spreadsheet software with the exception of (i) security.

A computer-based approach exposes the firm to threats from viruses, hackers and general system failure.

3   D

Budgeted production for a period = budgeted sales for the period − opening inventory of finished goods for the period + closing inventory of finished goods for the period.

Sales	F3
(Opening Inventory)	(10% F3)
Closing Inventory	10% F4
	————
Production	90% F3 + 10% F4

Or [(0.9*F3) + (0.1*F4)]

Index

Index

Index

Index